FORTRESS • 77

THE STALIN AND MOLOTOV LINES

Soviet Western Defences 1928–41

NEIL SHORT

ILLUSTRATED BY ADAM HOOK

Series editors Marcus Cowper and Nikolai Bogdanovic

First published in 2008 by Osprey Publishing
Midland House, West Way, Botley, Oxford OX2 0PH, UK
443 Park Avenue South, New York, NY 10016, USA
E-mail: info@ospreypublishing.com

ISBN-13: 978-184603-192-2

Editorial by Ilios Publishing, Oxford, UK (www.iliospublishing.com)
Cartography: Map Studio, Romsey, UK
Design: Ken Vail Graphic Design, Cambridge, UK (kvgd.com)
Typeset in Sabon and Myriad Pro
Index by Alan Thatcher
Originated by PDQ Digital Media Solutions Ltd, UK
Printed in China through Bookbuilders

08 09 10 11 12   10 9 8 7 6 5 4 3 2 1

A CIP catalogue record for this book is available from the British Library.

For a catalogue of all books published by Osprey Military and Aviation please contact:

Osprey Direct, c/o Random House Distribution Center, 400 Hahn Road, Westminster, MD 21157
Email: info@ospreydirect.com

Osprey Direct UK, P.O. Box 140, Wellingborough, Northants, NN8 2FA, UK
E-mail: info@ospreydirect.co.uk

www.ospreypublishing.com

ACKNOWLEDGEMENTS

Many people helped me in the production of this book and I would like to take this opportunity to thank each and every one. In particular, I would like to thank Evgeny Hitriak, Ivan Volkov and Valery Tadra who provided me with valuable information and photographs and took time out to show me around the Stalin Line defences in modern-day Belarus. I would also like to thank Tom Idzikowski who provided a number of the drawings and acted as guide and chauffeur around the Molotov Line defences in Poland. I am also indebted to Steve Zaloga and Gordon Rottman for their help. Finally I would like to thank my family and especially my wife and daughter for their forbearance.

ARTIST'S NOTE

Readers may care to note that the original paintings from which the colour plates in this book were prepared are available for private sale. All reproduction copyright whatsoever is retained by the Publishers. All enquiries should be addressed to:

Scorpio Gallery, PO Box 475, Hailsham, East Sussex, BN27 2SL, UK

The Publishers regret that they can enter into no correspondence upon this matter.

THE FORTRESS STUDY GROUP (FSG)

The object of the FSG is to advance the education of the public in the study of all aspects of fortifications and their armaments, especially works constructed to mount or resist artillery. The FSG holds an annual conference in September over a long weekend with visits and evening lectures, an annual tour abroad lasting about eight days, and an annual Members' Day.

The FSG journal *FORT* is published annually, and its newsletter *Casemate* is published three times a year. Membership is international. For further details, please contact:

The Secretary, c/o 6 Lanark Place, London, W9 1BS, UK

Website: www.fsgfort.com

THE WOODLAND TRUST

Osprey Publishing are supporting the Woodland Trust, the UK's leading woodland conservation charity, by funding the dedication of trees.

AUTHOR'S NOTE

One point worthy of note concerns translations from the Cyrillic alphabet. These can be rendered in a number of ways so it is possible to see a number of derivations of the same place name or term. For example, the River Dnepr can also be written as Dniepr or Dnieper. Wherever possible the author has attempted to be consistent throughout this work. The all too numerous conflicts of the 20th century, especially in Eastern Europe, also led to numerous border alterations which in turn saw places renamed, often a number of times, for example, Lvov (Lviv) in the Ukraine, which in Polish is Lwów and in German Lemberg. The place names have, wherever possible, been quoted in Russian with the alternative(s) in brackets.

CONTENTS

SOVIET WESTERN DEFENCES 1928–41

INTRODUCTION

Throughout history fortifications have played a pivotal role in protecting the strategic interests of the Soviet Union and its predecessor Tsarist Russia. In the 18th century work began on a series of defences on the Baltic, the best known of which was the great citadel of Kronstadt that protected St Petersburg. At the same time the coastline of the Crimea was fortified and the defences of Sevastopol played an important role in the fighting of the Crimean War, which raged from 1853 to 1856. Half a century later the defences around Port Arthur, the Russian naval base in Manchuria, proved to be a far tougher proposition than anticipated by the attacking Japanese and were to provide a taster of what was to come in World War I a decade later. However, the Russians (and the kingdoms that dominated the region before they were absorbed into the empire) had an even longer tradition of constructing castles and fortresses along the main invasion routes from the west. Towns and cities like Kingisepp, Ostrov, Pskov and Sebezh were fortified against attacks from, among others,

The fortress at Kamenets Podolski in the Ukraine. It successfully held out against attacks from Turks and Tartars. Defences have existed on the site since the Middle Ages. Later Soviet engineers established a fortified region to protect this strategically important position. (P. Netesov, courtesy of E Hitriak and I Volkov)

the Teutonic Knights, the Poles and the Swedes. This tradition continued into the 19th century when Warsaw was fortified, as was Brest, the largest fortress of the Russian Empire in that period.

In World War I the great fortresses of Warsaw and Brest were captured almost without a fight as the Central Powers advanced against the poorly equipped and ineptly led Russian Army. Later in the war the Russians did enjoy some limited success, but it proved to be too little too late. The Tsarist regime was overthrown and the new Bolshevik government sued for peace. This turn of events was greeted with consternation in the west and soon 'White Russians', backed by Russia's former allies (principally Britain and France), attempted to wrest power from Lenin and his cohorts. In the Civil War that followed, Trotsky's Red Army created a series of fortified regions, or *ukreplinnyje rajony*, to protect the new government's power base around Moscow and St Petersburg. These were often little more than field works, but these defences played an important part in securing victory for the Red Army.

The value of these defences in the Russian Civil War informed the debate on the shape of future defences much as the experiences of the main belligerents in World War I influenced their thinking on fortifications in the inter-war period. In the Soviet Union the outcome of these deliberations was a decision to create a series of fortified regions made up of pillboxes and bunkers to protect strategic interests. However, even such a relatively conservative undertaking was impossible in the period after the war because the Soviet economy was so weak.

In 1928 work on the western border defences finally began, but with funds limited the programme was restricted to four fortified regions. Later, as the economy grew more resources became available and it was decided to build a further nine fortified regions, which stretched the entire length of the frontier. Thereafter the building programme slowed, but with the rise of Nazism and the almost inexorable drift to war, the building programme was revitalized and in 1938 eight further fortified regions were commissioned to plug significant gaps in the line. However, the signing of the Nazi–Soviet Non Aggression Pact in 1939 and the subsequent partition of Poland rendered the defences of the Stalin Line obsolete. Most of the building work was stopped and the defences were abandoned in favour of a plan to build new fortifications along the revised border, the so-called Molotov Line.

It is worth pausing at this point to consider further the names of these defences. Firstly, although both are referred to as 'lines' the defences were not continuous, and as Alan Clark notes in his classic study of the war on the Eastern Front, *Barbarossa*, 'the term line, although it may have denoted an ultimate goal, was, in 1941, no more than a geographical illusion founded on the presence of a sequence of fortified districts all in roughly the same longitude'. Secondly, the names of the lines, although widely accepted today and used throughout this text and indeed in the title, were a western invention in keeping with the grandiose titles afforded defences in the rest of continental Europe (Maginot Line, West Wall etc.).

The first line of defences were named after the Soviet leader, although it is not clear how Stalin viewed this 'honour', and certainly not after the defences had been breached in the summer of 1941. The new border defences constructed in 1940/41 were, following the war, named after the Soviet Foreign Minister, presumably in acknowledgement of the fact that the fortifications had been constructed along the new border agreed by Vyacheslav Molotov. However, in the Soviet Union the defences were always described as fortified regions (*ukreplinnyje rajony*).

CHRONOLOGY

1917	October	October Revolution.
	December	Civil War starts.
1918	March	Treaty of Brest-Litovsk.
1919	February	Russo-Polish War.
1921	March	Treaty of Riga (peace with Poland).
1922		Civil War ends (although most of the fighting was over by 1920).
	April	Treaty of Rapallo – restoration of diplomatic and economic links between Soviet Union and Germany.
1924	January	Death of Lenin.
1927		'War alarm'.
1928		Work begins on the Stalin Line. First Five-Year Plan.
1933		Second Five-Year Plan.
1936		Spanish Civil War.
	August	Soviet Union begins supply of war *matériel*.
1938		Third Five-Year Plan. New URs created to fill gaps in line.
	March	German *Anschluss* with Austria.
	September	Munich peace agreement.
	October	Germany occupies Sudetenland.
1939	March	Bohemia and Moravia become German Protectorates. Memel Land returned to Germany.
	August	Nazi–Soviet Pact signed.
	1 September	Germany invades Poland.
	3 September	France and Great Britain declare war on Germany.
	November	Russo-Finnish (Winter) War.
1940	May	Peace of Moscow ending war with Finland. Germany launches offensive in west.
	22 June	France signs armistice with Germany.
	July	Baltic states annexed by Soviet Union and Bessarabia and Northern Bukovina annexed.
	Summer	Work begins in earnest on Molotov Line.
1941	January	Zhukov/Pavlov war game.
	May	NKO orders defences to be put on war footing.
	22 June	Germany invades USSR.
	29 June	Minsk captured.
	30 June	Brest fortress falls (although elements fight on into July).
	19 September	Kiev captured.

DESIGN AND DEVELOPMENT

It is impossible to talk about the defences of the Stalin and Molotov Lines without making reference to the physical geography of the western border area. Perhaps the most obvious feature is the enormous length of the frontier, which when work on the Stalin started in late 1927 stretched from the Gulf of Finland in the north to the Black Sea in the south. A little over a decade later, following the annexation of eastern Poland, the border was moved west and was extended so that it stretched some 4,500km.

The Stalin Line

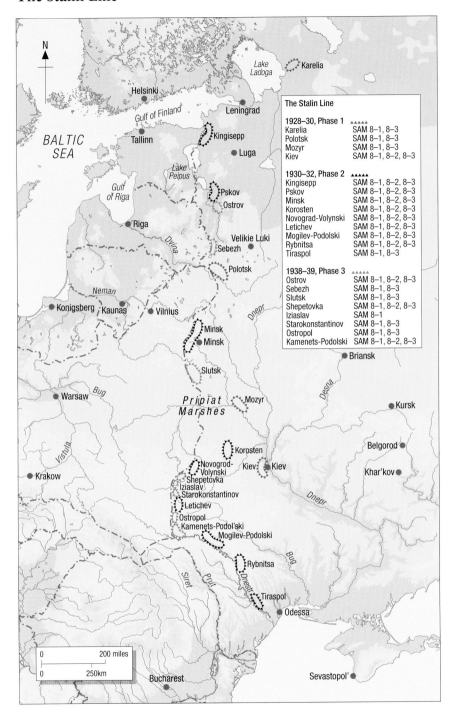

The Stalin Line

1928–30, Phase 1 ▲▲▲▲▲	
Karelia	SAM 8–1, 8–3
Polotsk	SAM 8–1, 8–3
Mozyr	SAM 8–1, 8–3
Kiev	SAM 8–1, 8–2, 8–3

1930–32, Phase 2 ▲▲▲▲▲	
Kingisepp	SAM 8–1, 8–2, 8–3
Pskov	SAM 8–1, 8–2, 8–3
Minsk	SAM 8–1, 8–2, 8–3
Korosten	SAM 8–1, 8–2, 8–3
Novograd-Volynski	SAM 8–1, 8–2, 8–3
Letichev	SAM 8–1, 8–2, 8–3
Mogilev-Podolski	SAM 8–1, 8–2, 8–3
Rybnitsa	SAM 8–1, 8–2, 8–3
Tiraspol	SAM 8–1, 8–3

1938–39, Phase 3 ▲▲▲▲▲	
Ostrov	SAM 8–1, 8–2, 8–3
Sebezh	SAM 8–1, 8–3
Slutsk	SAM 8–1, 8–3
Shepetovka	SAM 8–1, 8–2, 8–3
Iziaslav	SAM 8–1
Starokonstantinov	SAM 8–1, 8–3
Ostropol	SAM 8–1, 8–3
Kamenets-Podolski	SAM 8–1, 8–2, 8–3

The Stalin Line ran broadly from the Gulf of Finland in the north to the Black Sea in the south. Rather than a continuous line, the defences were built as series of fortified regions each of which covered a strategically important area of the border. It was built in three stages – four fortified regions in the first phase beginning in 1928, then a further nine were begun in the early 1930s and finally another batch of eight was started in 1938.

Neatly bisecting the frontier zone are the Pripiat Marshes, a vast tract of swamp and forest, more than 300km across. Throughout history this feature has been a major obstacle for any potential aggressor, but the marshes have also played an important part in the defensive thinking of the Russians and never more so than in the 20th century. Because they are all but impassable to a modern mechanized army, this portion of the front only needed to be lightly defended. But the marshes also effectively meant that the Red Army would have to be split in two, with one half covering Moscow and Leningrad to the north and the other half the major food-producing regions to the south. Moreover, because road and rail links through this area were poor or non-existent these two forces would have to operate independently.

Elsewhere, east–west communication links were better, although there were relatively few major, metalled roads. The border zone was, however, well served by rail links that were extended into Poland after 1939. These were broad gauge and provided the Soviet Army with a valuable advantage over any potential aggressor, because the enemy would either have to modify the entire rail network or they would have to capture sufficient engines and rolling stock from the Soviets to enable the system to be used.

To facilitate any attack an invading force would also need to secure the bridges over the many rivers that criss-cross the western border region. These are wide and fast flowing and crucially for the Soviets they often ran across the path of any potential invading army advancing from the west. As such they provided a useful barrier around which to organize the Red Army's defence and many of the fortifications were anchored on rivers or other water features.

It was with this background that the Soviet military engineers put their minds to fortifying the border. Their thinking, as elsewhere in Europe, was coloured by their experiences in World War I, but more significantly by the fighting in the Civil War that raged from end of 1917 until 1922. There were a number of reasons for this. Firstly, unlike on the Western Front where the forts of Verdun had been the keystone of the French defence, fortresses played a relatively small role in the fighting in the east. The Austro-Hungarian forts around the city of Przemysl were besieged and captured by the Russians in the early part of the war and the Germans quickly seized the Russian fortresses at Warsaw and Brest. Secondly, many officers of the Russian Army who had served in World War I were either dead or in exile, having fought with the White Russians against the Bolsheviks, and as such the Red Army could not benefit from their experiences. By contrast the lessons learned in the fighting of the Civil War were more immediate and more easily distilled.

The Russian Civil War

One of the bunkers built in 1928 in response to the 'war alarm'. This example is a two-storey machine-gun bunker that formed part of the Polotsk Fortified Region. The bunker was destroyed during the war. (Author's photograph)

During the struggle against the foreign-backed counter-revolutionary forces, the 'Workers and Peasants Red Army' (Robochiy Krestyanskaya Krasnaya Armiya – RKKA), or Red Army, created a series of fortified regions (*ukreplinnyje rajony* – UR). These defences were designed not only to protect the fledgling socialist state but were also to act as jumpingoff points for offensive operations. With little in the way of raw materials and no industrial base to build permanent fortifications, these positions consisted of little more than field works and were constructed using the one resource they did have – manpower. By the end of the Civil War, 45 of these fortified regions had been completed, but with the disappearance of the threat from the foreign-backed White Russians these were largely abandoned and the government concentrated on industrial and agricultural reform. However, the value of such defences was recognized.

The first building phase – war alarm

After the Civil War relations with the west gradually thawed, driven in no small part by commercial interest in exploiting the vast Soviet market. Nevertheless, there was still concern in the capitalist west at the subversive activities of the Soviets, who supported political extremists all over the world. As the Soviet economy recovered, fears grew in London and Paris that this strength would be used to restore the Red Army and that the Soviet Union would threaten the independence of the small states on its border. The western democracies therefore looked to strengthen the 'small Entente' states (Estonia, Latvia, Lithuania, Poland, Romania and Finland) against possible aggression. This intervention discomfited the Bolshevik government, because although neither Britain nor France had a common border with the Soviet Union their involvement in these countries offered them another opportunity to destabilize or even overthrow the government. In truth there was never ever any real prospect of an invasion, but the perceived threat, which came to its height in 1927 with the so called 'war alarm' (Moscow was convinced that Britain was encouraging the Soviet Union's neighbours to launch a land attack while the Royal Navy would impose a blockade), was enough to convince a paranoid Soviet leadership that steps needed to be taken to counter it.

As a first step the General Staff of the Red Army proposed the building of a series of fortified regions similar to those used so successfully in the Civil War. The idea was driven by a number of considerations. Firstly, poor communication links meant that the Red Army took longer to mobilize than its neighbours (some of the most developed sections of the rail network had been lost with the redrawing of the border after World War I and the Polish–Soviet War, and in spite of great efforts to develop the network work was still far from complete). As such it was necessary to have defences in place to slow an enemy advance and provide breathing space. Secondly, it was prompted by the shape of the threat that was considered to face the Soviet Union, that is, a co-ordinated attack from the Baltic States, Poland, Finland and Romania, backed by Britain and France. By constructing fortified regions in key areas it would be possible to hold the front with a reduced force, thus freeing up units to deliver a crushing blow against each of the aggressors in turn.

Thus in 1927 the decision was taken to build four fortified regions (URs). The Karelia UR was to be built in the Leningrad Military District (MD) and would protect Leningrad, an industrial centre, but also symbolically the birthplace of the Revolution, from attack by Finland. Two further fortified regions were to be constructed in the Belorussian MD. The Polotsk UR covered the River Daugava and the strategic rail junction on the border with Poland and Latvia and also blocked the route to Smolensk and ultimately Moscow. The Mozyr UR protected the rail, road and river links that were concentrated around the city and blocked one of the key avenues of attack out of Poland. The Kiev UR would protect the Ukrainian capital with an arc of defences anchored at each end on the River Dnieper. It was also suggested that fortified regions should be built at Pskov and Lepel (on the highway between Vitebsk and Minsk), but this work was not started.

In the summer of 1928 the new chief of staff, B.M. Shaposhnikov, asked for 40 million roubles for the construction programme, but K.E. Voroshilov, the People's Commissar for Military and Navy Affairs and Chairman of the Revolutionary Military Council of the USSR, could only afford 24 million roubles. With a typical machine-gun pillbox costing in the region of

Table 1: Stalin Line – the first building phase

Fortified region	Start date	Finish date	Cost, million Rubles
Karelia	1928	1932	9.8[1]
Polotsk	1930[2]	1932	7.8
Mozyr	1931	1932	5.2
Kiev	1929	1932	9.1

Notes:

[1] Not definitive. In all likelihood the defences cost much more.

[2] Although a number of installations were built in 1927–28.

30,000–40,000 roubles, this constraint meant a significant reduction in the number of fortifications that could be built. However, in the end the purse strings were eased and around 32 million roubles were spent on the defences (see Table 1).

The second building phase
Agricultural and industrial reform saw the Soviet economy strengthen and grow, and this gathered pace after the introduction of the first Five-Year Plan in 1928. In the fullness of time this and later plans would deliver the industrial strength to create a powerful Red Army. In the meantime a decision was taken to expand the fortifications programme with the construction of a further nine fortified regions which brought the total to 13.

The majority of the defences were concentrated in the Ukraine with seven fortified regions located in the Kiev MD to protect the vital industrial and agricultural centres in the area. Kiev itself was already protected by a band of defences on the city's western fringes and was now further protected by the Korosten, Novograd-Volynski and Letichev URs that provided an outer screen of defences, running from the Pripiat Marshes to the River Bug, against a possible Polish incursion. On either side of this military district further defences were built to protect cities close to the border or to block possible invasion routes. To the south the Mogilev-Podolski, Rybnitsa and Tiraspol URs, which ran along the eastern bank of the River Dniester, protected the border, and the vital naval base at Odessa, against a possible attack from Romania.

To the north the Kingisepp UR, which ran along the eastern bank of the River Narva and was anchored in the north on the Baltic Sea and to the south by Lake Peipus, protected Leningrad from any attack from the west. Meantime the Pskov UR, which ran south from Lake Pskov along the River Velikaya, protected the city against an attack from the south-west (both Kingisepp and Pskov were technically *ukreplinnyje polosa* – UP – or fortified zones). Further south in the Western MD, the Minsk UR protected the Belorussian capital and partially plugged the gap between the Polotsk and Mozyr fortified regions.

The third building phase
During the course of the 1930s the political map of Europe changed, and with it the threat to the Soviet Union. Britain and France now accepted the socialist regime and had enjoyed intermittently good relations with Moscow. Far more worrying, however, was the resurgence of an emboldened Germany.

Already in 1936 Hitler had remilitarized the Rhineland and in 1938 Germany forged an *Anschluss* with Austria and absorbed the Czech Sudetenland into the greater Reich. These developments prompted the Soviets to institute a new building programme. This drew on the lessons they had learned in the Spanish Civil War, where they advised the forces of the Republican government. The internecine fighting had clearly demonstrated that in spite of the rapid development of mechanized forces, the ability of this new arm to deliver a decisive victory was more limited than originally envisaged. The Soviets believed that the offensive would once again be dominated by artillery with tanks supporting the infantry. Indeed, if anything, it seemed that developments in weaponry since World War I had strengthened the defender. Well-prepared defences like those of the Ebro Line could only be breached through the relentless pressure of artillery, tanks and infantry (or, as in the case of the 'Iron Ring' around Bilbao – a series of concrete emplacements and fieldworks that

The Molotov Line

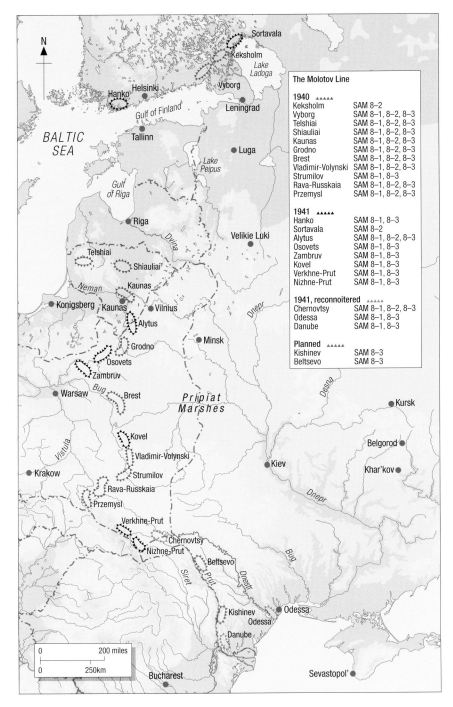

The Molotov Line was some 320km west of the Stalin Line and stretched from Lithuania, which had been absorbed into the Soviet Union in 1940, to the mouth of the Danube. Rather than one continuous line, it consisted of a number of fortified regions which were anything from 50 to 120km in length. It was started in 1940 and suspended in the winter of 1940 before recommencing in 1941.

The Molotov Line

1940 ▲▲▲▲▲
Keksholm	SAM 8–2
Vyborg	SAM 8–1, 8–2, 8–3
Telshiai	SAM 8–1, 8–2, 8–3
Shiauliai	SAM 8–1, 8–2, 8–3
Kaunas	SAM 8–1, 8–2, 8–3
Grodno	SAM 8–1, 8–2, 8–3
Brest	SAM 8–1, 8–2, 8–3
Vladimir-Volynski	SAM 8–1, 8–2, 8–3
Strumilov	SAM 8–1, 8–3
Rava-Russkaia	SAM 8–1, 8–2, 8–3
Przemysl	SAM 8–1, 8–2, 8–3

1941 ▲▲▲▲▲
Hanko	SAM 8–1, 8–3
Sortavala	SAM 8–2
Alytus	SAM 8–1, 8–2, 8–3
Osovets	SAM 8–1, 8–3
Zambruv	SAM 8–1, 8–3
Kovel	SAM 8–1, 8–3
Verkhne-Prut	SAM 8–1, 8–3
Nizhne-Prut	SAM 8–1, 8–3

1941, reconnoitered ▲▲▲▲▲
Chernovtsy	SAM 8–1, 8–2, 8–3
Odessa	SAM 8–1, 8–3
Danube	SAM 8–1, 8–3

Planned ▲▲▲▲▲
Kishinev	SAM 8–3
Beltsevo	SAM 8–3

formed an 80km defensive perimeter – by treachery). Based on this experience the Soviets planned to build a further eight fortified regions along the length of the front and these would be built in even greater depth.

This new building programme was once again concentrated in the Kiev MD with the creation of the Shepetovka, Iziaslavl, Starokonstantinov, Ostropol and Kamenets-Podolski URs. These plugged the gaps between the existing fortified districts and now produced an almost continuous outer line of defences around the Ukrainian capital. Two further fortified regions were created in the Leningrad Special MD at Ostrov and Sebezh. These were designed to fill the gaps between the Pskov and Polotsk URs along the Latvian border, which Stalin viewed as a possible conduit for German troops advancing from East Prussia (in October 1940 the Pskov and Ostrov URs were merged). Finally, a fortified region was established in front of Slutsk that continued the Minsk defences further south to the Pripiat Marshes.

The Soviets also took the opportunity to strengthen some of the original fortified regions. The Polotsk UR was to be reinforced with the addition of 45 new emplacements while in the Korosten UR 14 new artillery positions were planned. At the same time (July 1938) the heightened tension led to a reappraisal of the status of the various military districts. Both the Belorussian and Kiev MDs were given the prefix 'special' (*osobyi*), which signified that the district was being brought up to a higher readiness level in order to meet the increased threat.

The Molotov Line

A secret protocol to the Nazi–Soviet Non Aggression Pact (or Molotov–Ribbentrop Pact) of August 1939 effectively removed Poland from the political map. This shifted the Soviet border 200–400km west and in so doing recovered the territory lost to the Soviet Union in the first few years after the Revolution. It was unquestionably Stalin's most notable diplomatic success to date. This new swathe of territory not only shifted the border away from some of the major western cities, but also provided an ideal jumping-off point for a pre-emptive attack – the Red Army's westernmost forces were now closer to Berlin than to Moscow. By the same token, the Soviet Union now no longer had a border with Poland, but with its ideological enemy Nazi Germany. The most serious consequence of this change was that previously an attack by the Germans through Poland would have given the Red Army due warning and time to mobilize behind the Stalin Line, but now no buffer zone existed.

A drawing of a unique position in the Molotov Line mounting four machine guns and two 45mm anti-tank guns – three weapons on each side. The position was one of six bunkers in the Stare Brusno Position, which was part of the Rava-Russkaia Fortified Region. (T. Idzikowski)

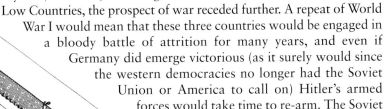

Yet in the winter of 1939 the prospect of invasion was a remote possibility with Germany embroiled in a war with France and Great Britain (albeit a phoney war). In 1940, following the German invasion of France and the Low Countries, the prospect of war receded further. A repeat of World War I would mean that these three countries would be engaged in a bloody battle of attrition for many years, and even if Germany did emerge victorious (as it surely would since the western democracies no longer had the Soviet Union or America to call on) Hitler's armed forces would take time to re-arm. The Soviet Union was then seemingly safe from attack and Stalin took the opportunity to fully assimilate his territorial gains.

Part of this process included a decision to fortify the new border. Two alternatives were presented: fortifications could either be built right along the new frontier, or slightly further to the rear. The latter had a number of advantages, not the least of which was that the defences could be built out of sight of the enemy. Also, the buffer zone, if sewn with mines and obstacles, would delay the enemy and enable troops of the first echelon to man the defences and allow reserves to be mobilized.

Shaposhnikov, who was Chief of the General Staff at that time, certainly favoured this approach and indeed went further, suggesting that the main body of the Red Army should be positioned behind the Stalin Line and that only a screening force should be deployed in the newly occupied territories. However, Stalin would not countenance such an approach. He would not allow these territories to be lost and impressed on Shaposhnikov the need to defend this territory against any possible invasion. To Stalin, building fortifications along the new border would ensure that his gains were not lost. And yet, paradoxically, by building defences along the new border and holding the bulk of his forces in forward positions he increased the chance of the very thing he hoped to avoid happening.

A Maxim 1910 machine gun mounted on a PSK-2 gun carriage. This rested on a roller which ran along a track to enable the gun to be traversed. A hand wheel was used to raise and lower the weapon. Exhaust fumes were vented through rubber hoses. (Soviet Archives)

Whilst the debate about the location of the defences had been resolved, their make-up had not. General Khrenov, who headed the Main Military Engineering Directorate (Glavnoe Voenno-inzhenernoe Upravleniia), suggested that rather than permanent works, effort should be concentrated on the construction of field works, with particular emphasis on blocking potential invasion routes with obstacles. Then, if time allowed, a second phase of building would be instituted with the construction of permanent defences. However, his plan was not adopted and instead a comprehensive building programme for the construction of thousands of concrete bunkers and pillboxes was developed, much to his *chagrin*.

As work on the plans for the new border defences began, Stalin, fresh from his coup in the west, attempted to flex his muscles with another neighbour. In the autumn of 1939 negotiations with Finland about adjustments to their common border and the creation of naval bases on Finnish territory broke down and in November a border incident precipitated the outbreak of war. Stalin believed that the Finns would offer little resistance, but it was not until March 1940 that they finally capitulated, and only after they had inflicted a series of embarrassing defeats on their much larger neighbour. Part of the reason for these reversals, aside from Soviet ineptitude, was the defences of the Mannerheim Line. Named after Marshal Carl Mannerheim, the Finnish Commander in Chief, the line was made up of a series of gun emplacements, trenches and obstacles constructed in depth that blunted the Soviet attacks.

The experience of the Soviet Army in Finland seemed to reaffirm the value of fixed fortifications, and was one of the few positives to emerge from the short and bloody campaign. Another was the territory that Finland was forced to cede to the Soviet Union under the terms of the Peace of Moscow signed by both nations following the cessation of fighting in May 1940. This included a number of pieces of land on the Karelian Isthmus including Sortavala, Keksholm and Vyborg as well the Hanko (Hangö) Peninsula – a strategically important headland that jutted out into the Baltic Sea and protected the seaborne approaches to Leningrad. Almost immediately these areas, along with Murmansk, were fortified and formed part of the western defences.

In that same month a report was written describing the progress of the border defences. This concluded that, 'preparation of the theatres of military operations for war is extremely poor in all respects' (Tarleton, 1993, p.40). Yet no sooner had this report been published than the whole value of fortifications was cast into doubt with the stunning German victories in the west. Neither the Maginot Line, nor the defences in Belgium and Holland, proved to be any match for the German Wehrmacht. In part at least this poor showing was put down to the fact that the Germans had attacked an incomplete section of the Maginot Line that covered the border with Belgium. The Soviets would not make the same mistake and while Hitler contemplated an invasion of Britain, Stalin took the opportunity to consolidate his hold in the east.

In the autumn of 1939 the Baltic states had entered into a military alliance with the Soviet Union and in the summer of the following year the puppet governments of Estonia, Latvia and Lithuania asked to be absorbed into the Soviet Union. To protect this territory a new Baltic Special Military District was created and in the spring of 1941 work commenced on the Telshiai, Shiauliai, Kaunas and Alytus URs, which ran from the Baltic Sea along the border with East Prussia to the old Lithuanian border. With little in the way of natural features – save for the River Bug right on the border – engineers were forced to construct defences along the entire frontier.

Similarly, in the summer of 1940 pressure was applied to the Romanian government to cede Bessarabia and Northern Bukovina to the Soviet Union, which it did following advice from Berlin. Now the boundary of the Odessa MD was pushed even further west to the banks of the River Danube and the Prut. Further defences were planned along the River Prut to reinforce those already constructed along the Dniester, but the Beltsevo and Kishinev URs did not progress beyond the drawing board.

The main construction effort was concentrated in the Western Special Military District, which replaced the Belorussian Special Military District as of 11 July 1940. In the summer of 1940 work began on the Grodno and Brest fortified regions, which protected the flanks of the Bialystok salient, and in the following spring work began on a further two fortified regions – Osovets and Zambruv – to produce a solid line of defences around the bulge. In the summer of 1940 work also began on new fortifications in the Kiev Special MD with construction of defences in the Vladimir-Volynski, Strumilov, Rava-Russkaia and Przemysl fortified regions. In the following year work started on further defences at either end of the military district with the establishment of the Kovel Fortified Region to the north and the Verkhne Prut and Nizhne Prut fortified regions to the south. Preparatory work also began in the Odessa MD on the Chernovtsy, Danube (Dunayskiy) and Odessa fortified regions, which were designed to deter any attack from Romania.

The value of the new border defences was called into further question by a war game in January 1941 between General Zhukov, then commander of the Kiev Special MD, and Colonel General D.G. Pavlov, the commander of the Western Special MD, which demonstrated the folly of building the fortifications along the vast winding frontier. Zhukov was able to thrust deep into Belorussia, and he argued that part of the reason for this was the thin band of fortifications around the Bialystok salient. These failed to adequately protect the troops positioned there, leaving them vulnerable to encirclement. His comments were not welcomed by Marshal K.E. Voroshilov and Pavlov. Yet in spite of this, on the very next day, he was made Chief of the General Staff and became responsible for the western border defences, the value of which he had just questioned.

One of the first issues he had to address was the increased demand for resources necessitated by the extensive building programme. To meet these needs work on all but one of the eight fortified regions in the Stalin Line that was still progressing when Poland was annexed was suspended (work continued on the Kamenets-Podolski UR along the River Dniester on the border with Romania) – a decision if not made by Stalin then certainly known by him. It was also suggested that the shortage of weapons could be solved by redirecting weapons originally destined for the Stalin Line to the new border defences. Zhukov and Marshal S.K. Timoshenko objected to this proposal, partly because they believed that these weapons would be quickly lost in any German invasion and partly because the weapons were not suited to the new emplacements, but they also believed that a fully armed Stalin Line had some use. Nevertheless, their objections were overruled by Stalin.

In spite of this setback, Zhukov and Timoshenko took tentative steps to restore the old Stalin Line, and this plan gained added urgency as rumours of a possible German invasion gained credence. In April Zhukov ordered that the Stalin Line be readied for war and when the strength of the Red Army was increased in June a small number of troops were allocated to man the old defences. That same month Zhukov also ordered that the fortifications on the border be equipped with whatever weapons were at hand and that armoured doors be fitted to protect their crews. This was to take priority over work to install communication links, power and efforts to protect the shelters against gas attack. This burst of energy meant that by the time of the German invasion 2,300 strongpoints had been completed. But the statistics could not disguise the fact that more than half of these emplacements were only armed with machine guns; nor were the positions integrated, but rather were a series of individual strongpoints that had little or no camouflage and also lacked minefields and obstacles.

THE PRINCIPLES OF DEFENCE

The strategic level

To the Russians the primacy of the offensive was an article of faith. This was exemplified in the battle plans developed before the outbreak of World War I that called for immediate, simultaneous offensives against both Germany and Austria. Ultimately this strategy led to disaster with the defeat of the Russian Army, but more significantly the overthrow of the Tsar and the seizure of power by Lenin's Bolsheviks. The new socialist regime was soon on the defensive as White Russian forces, backed by a number of foreign powers including Britain and France, tried to overthrow the government. However, this disparate force was never able to co-ordinate its attacks, and the Red Army gradually grew in strength and confidence and defeated each of the opposing armies in turn. In 1920 the Bolshevik government had sufficient faith in the Red Army's abilities to launch an attack on Poland in an effort to regain the territory lost after World War I. Mikhail Tukhachevskii, a former Tsarist officer, led the counter-strike. His background and training meant he was still very much wedded to the idea of the primacy of the offensive, and this together with the Bolsheviks' desire to export their revolutionary ideas abroad was a powerful combination. However, in spite of this the campaign was an unmitigated disaster and the Bolsheviks were forced to sue for peace. There now followed a period of introspection as the government concentrated on the defence of the Soviet Union's borders and internal reform rather than global revolution.

In that same year, Fedor I. Golenkin, a major-general in World War I, recommended that a series of fortified zones be constructed along the western border – an idea that had already been used successfully in the Civil War. These defences would not only protect the country's borders, but would allow the Red Army to mobilize and also act as secure bases from which offensive operations could be launched. The possibility of using border defences as a springboard for offensive operations was also recognized by Lt-Gen Dmitry Karbyshev, the Red Army's leading expert on fortifications in the inter-war period, in a study he undertook in 1924. Initially, though, the weakened Soviet economy meant that it did not have the resources to build the defences or to maintain an army at high readiness levels, and the focus turned to more pressing issues like agricultural reform and industrialization.

By the end of the decade the position had improved and in 1928 the first work on the western defences began. Somewhat ironically Tukhachevskii, who had led the failed attack on Poland, was in overall control of the fortifications programme. He was still convinced of the primacy of the offensive and that trench warfare was a thing of the past. Yet in spite of this he recognized the value of fixed fortifications. He not only believed fortified regions could act as a shield which would absorb an enemy blow and provide the basis for a Red Army counterattack, but also that the defences had the potential to screen a possible Red Army mobilization which could deliver a pre-emptive strike against a Polish (or German) force massing in the west.

His ideas were incorporated in the *Provisional Field Service Regulations of the Worker and Peasants Red Army 1936*. In Chapter 8, which was dedicated to defence, it was noted that, 'defence, combined with offensive action or with a subsequent transition to the offensive, especially against the flank of a weakened enemy, can lead to his complete destruction' (Erickson, 2001, p.803).

After Tukhachevskii's demise (he was killed in June 1937 as part of Stalin's purge of the officer classes) Boris Shaposhnikov, the Chief of the General Staff, refined the idea and gave it form in his 1938 War Plan. This considered the two most likely routes of an enemy invasion: north of the Pripiat Marshes along the Minsk–Smolensk axis towards Moscow and to the south of this feature towards Kiev and the economically vital Ukraine. Both of these potential invasion routes were protected by fortified regions that were designed to slow down and weaken any invading force and allow the Red Army to mobilize and then go on the offensive.

Following the defeat and partition of Poland in October 1939 the Soviet frontier was moved some 200km to the west. Almost immediately work on the Stalin Line was suspended and the fortifications mothballed. Efforts were now concentrated on building new defences along the border with the Third Reich.

This change forced a major rethink of the Red Army's war plans and resulted in the October 1940 deployment plan, which in many ways was similar to that drawn up in 1938, but was now based around the Molotov Line. The defences of the fortified regions would be manned by the first strategic echelon, whose job it was to repulse the initial attack and allow the second echelon to mobilize and then drive the enemy back.

The October 1940 deployment plan was refined in early May 1941 in the *Plan for the Defence of the State Frontier 1941*. The success of this plan, like previous ones, was based on the assumption that a German build up would provide sufficient warning of an attack to enable the first echelon units to mobilize. These troops, ensconced in their fortifications, would hold the enemy sufficiently long to enable the second echelon to be brought to full readiness and deliver a decisive counter blow. No thought had been given to any other possible scenario.

The operational level

In realizing their strategic objectives the Soviets constructed a series of fortified regions both as part of the Stalin Line and later in the construction of the Molotov Line. Each fortified region was between 50 and 150km in length (although a number were even longer) and from 30 to 50km in depth and each had its own garrison. The fortified regions of both the Stalin and Molotov lines stretched almost the entire length of the border with gaps between the defences of 12 to 20km, which in time of war were to be defended by rifle divisions (save for a large gap in front of the Pripiat Marshes because it was rightly considered impenetrable for a modern mechanized army).

The fortified regions were built to protect major cities and vital industrial and agricultural areas or to block possible avenues of attack, and tended to be anchored on natural features like rivers. The defences in each of the fortified regions were constructed in depth with a series of defensive zones one behind the other. The theory behind the system was simple. As the enemy advanced through the zones it became weaker and weaker and was less able to maintain the momentum of the attack. At the same time the attackers moved beyond the range of their supporting artillery, leaving them dangerously exposed. Exhausted and isolated the enemy was vulnerable to counterattack from Soviet reserves which had been given time to fully mobilize.

The tactical level

The first four fortified regions built between 1928 and 1932 consisted of a forward defence zone, or *polosa obespecheniia* (sometimes termed *predpol'e*) some 10–12km in depth. This included obstacles and lightly fortified pillboxes that were designed to slow the enemy and dissipate their strength before they reached the main defensive zone. This was 3–4km deep and consisted of as many as six battalion defence regions (BDRs), or *batal'onnye raiony oborony*. Each of these was oval shaped and was 1.5–3km deep and twice as wide. They were constructed 5–8km apart in a chessboard pattern. The battalion defence region was in turn made up of a series of three to four company defence areas (CDAs), or *rotnyi uchastok oborony* (RUO) linked by a mixture of field works, trenches and obstacles. These company defence areas were also oval in shape and consisted of a number of concrete pillboxes and timber and earth bunkers, linked by communication trenches and protected by dragon's teeth, anti-tank ditches and wire. The equipment and the layout of the various defences were dictated by the strategic importance of the position. Smaller sectors of the front were protected by company defence regions (CDRs), or *rotnyi rayon oborony*. (RRO); these are not to be confused with company defence areas – the company defence region was often linked to a battalion defence region but was independent.

The later defences of the Stalin Line were arranged in much the same way, but were now constructed in greater depth to counter the threat from mechanized forces. The forward defence zone was extended to 12–18km and the main defence zone was similarly enlarged. The battalion defence region, which after 1938 was referred to as a 'centre of resistance', was 5–10km deep and a similar distance wide and consisted of three to five strongpoints, or *opornye punkty*, each again made up of a mixture of permanent defences and field works, trenches and obstacles. The defences of the Molotov Line were organized in much the same way as those of the later Stalin Line programme, but were to be built in even greater depth, although many were not completed.

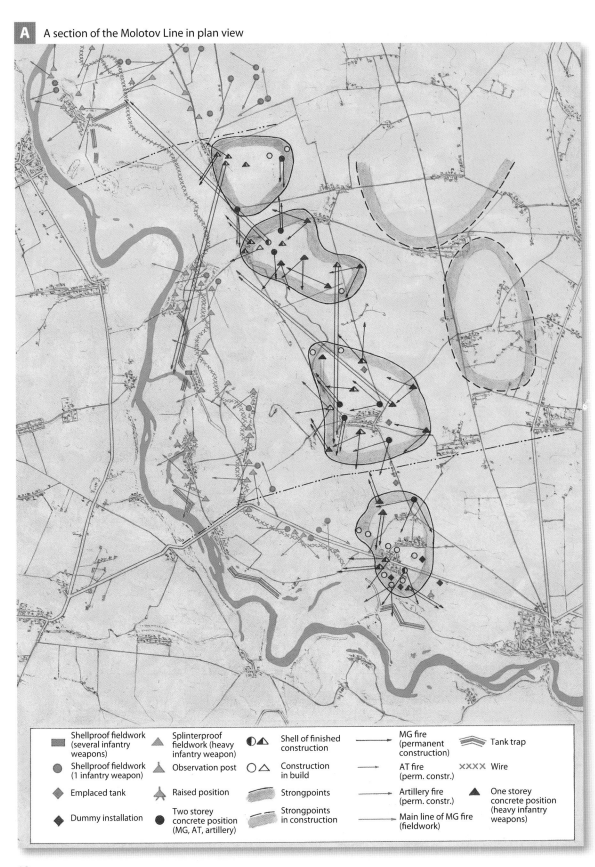

■	Shellproof fieldwork (several infantry weapons)	▲	Splinterproof fieldwork (heavy infantry weapon)	◐▲	Shell of finished construction	⟶ MG fire (permanent construction)	Tank trap
●	Shellproof fieldwork (1 infantry weapon)	⚑	Observation post	○△	Construction in build	⟶ AT fire (perm. constr.)	×××× Wire
◆	Emplaced tank	⚓	Raised position		Strongpoints	⟶ Artillery fire (perm. constr.)	▲ One storey concrete position (heavy infantry weapons)
◆	Dummy installation	●	Two storey concrete position (MG, AT, artillery)		Strongpoints in construction	⟶ Main line of MG fire (fieldwork)	

Almost immediately after the defeat of Poland in October 1939 Stalin set in train plans to fortify the new border with Hitler's Third Reich, defences that were later to become known as the Molotov Line. One of the most important sections of the new line was around the Bialystok salient that jutted into German-occupied Poland. This was extremely vulnerable to attack and as such was heavily fortified. The defences were constructed all along the border and often in full view of the Germans. The lower lip of the salient ran along the River Bug and on the far bank a series of fortifications were built as part of the Brest Fortified Region.

A typical section of the line ran north from the historic town of Drohiczyn, and is shown here. At the leading edge along the river were a series of outposts and passive anti-tank and anti-infantry obstacles including tank traps and barbed wire. Behind these were a number of 'centres of resistance' (before 1938 these were referred to as battalion defence regions) along the main defence line that consisted of as many as five strongpoints in a chessboard pattern. Each strongpoint was 2–3 km wide and a similar depth. These were made up of a series of mutually supporting bunkers and field works armed with a mixture of machine guns, anti-tank guns and artillery.

A TOUR OF THE DEFENCES

In the Russian Civil War the majority of the defences constructed by the Red Army had been field works. These were quick to construct and provided adequate protection for the troops, but they were not suitable for the new building programme. Firstly, to protect troops against modern ordnance these earth and timber constructions would have to be so large as to be easily seen by the enemy. Secondly, timber shelters tended to rot away in a few years and these defences were needed for the long term. The solution was to build shelters from the new high-strength reinforced concrete that had been developed in World War I.

The Department for the Construction of Permanent Defensive Installations (Otdel Stroitelstva Kapitalnyh Oboronitelnyh Soorujenii) completed the first bunker designs. Initially these shelters were not given specific names, but instead were described in narrative, for example, 'concrete machine gun pillbox for three MGs', and often there was further detail explaining whether the shelter had one or two storeys. Four experimental bunkers were constructed during the winter of 1927/28 in the Polotsk UR. Among them were designs by I.O. Belinskii who had developed the 'fortress forest' concept in the 1920s, which involved planting a thick belt of trees and thorny bushes along the border that would be impassable to the enemy.

It was not until 1929 that the first step in classifying the bunkers was taken with the introduction of three standard types: 'A' type – a two-storey construction with gas shelter that provided protection against 203mm howitzer

BELOW LEFT
A destroyed bunker in the Polotsk Fortified Region of the Stalin Line. This was one of the original bunkers built in 1928 and constructed over two storeys. The two loopholes are just visible and the recesses are reinforced with steel plate that has been riveted and bolted into place. (Author's photograph)

BELOW RIGHT
A battalion command post in the Minsk Fortified Region. The position was armed with three Maxim machine guns. The bunker would not have been as exposed as it is today – the line of the original soil level is just visible below the loopholes. (Author's photograph)

RIGHT
Bunker No. 160a of Battalion Defence Area VI in the Minsk Fortified Region. This is a 'Moskit' bunker armed with a single machine gun; these were often built to provide additional defence for the larger bunkers. These bunkers had an 'a' or 'b' suffix because they were often constructed after the main bunkers had been finished. (V. Tadra)

OPPOSITE PAGE, TOP LEFT
The entrance to a battalion command post in the Minsk Fortified Region. The main entrance is to the right and would have been secured with a steel gate and covered by an internal loophole. The opening to the left is slightly smaller and was designed to dissipate the explosive force of a charge placed near the solid steel door inside. (Author's photograph)

OPPOSITE PAGE, TOP RIGHT
A wooden Gornostalev carriage used to mount a Maxim machine gun. Just visible on the base plate is a semicircular rule that enabled the gunner to know how far he had traversed the gun. Fitted to the wooden mount was a simple seat that could be adjusted for height. This example in mounted in a bunker in the Minsk Fortified Region. (Author's photograph)

shells/152mm artillery shells; 'B' type – a single-storey construction with gas shelter which provided protection against 152mm artillery shells; and 'O' type – a single-storey construction with no gas shelter that provided protection against 152mm artillery shells.

In 1930 a further class was introduced with the addition of the 'M' type and in the following year the classification system was streamlined with bunkers now divided into three types (the old 'A' and 'B' types were reclassified as 'B' type and the old 'O' and 'M' types were reclassified as 'M' type): 'B' type (from the Russian *Bolshoy* – big) – one/two-storey construction with technical room and living quarters (which often formed the headquarters for the machine-gun battalions; 'M' type (from the Russian *maliy* – small) – single-storey construction with two or more loopholes and an observation /command post but with no technical room or living quarters; and 'MS' type – single-storey construction with one loophole. At the same time a system for classifying the strength of the bunkers was introduced (see Table 2).

After 1938 the classes of protection were dispensed with and instead bunkers were given numbers according to the protection that the shelter offered against guns of a certain calibre. In addition to being classified by strength the bunkers were also classified according to their role, for example: fighting post – *boyevoe sooruzheniye*; observation post – *nabludatelnyi punkt*; command post – *komandnyi punkt*; anti-tank firing post – *protivotankovaya ognevaya tochka*; or shelter – *ubezhische*.

Table 2: Bunker classification					
Class	Front wall (mm)	Roof (mm)	Base (mm)	Rear wall (mm)	Protection (range 6km)
M1	150	110	70	80	203mm howitzer/152mm artillery
M2	135	90	60	60	152mm howitzer/artillery
M3	90	60	50	50	122mm howitzer/76mm artillery

Notes:
Sometimes a fourth classification was used. The M4 shelter was different to the other shelters. It came in two forms: a light MG pillbox and a dummy construction designed to deceive the enemy. The light MG shelter or 'Moskit' (literally Mosquito) was armed with a single machine gun and was constructed in the outpost zone and would be the first to engage the enemy. When their position had been identified the crew would retreat to the main defensive zone. The M4 'Masket' – often confused with the 'Moskit' or MS shelter – was a simple pillbox with no equipment, or sometimes a concrete wall with loophole that looked to the enemy like a genuine position.

The fighting posts were also given further descriptions depending on their direction of fire: frontal firing – *ognevaya tochka;* flank (both directions) – caponier; flank (one direction) – half caponier; or all-round fire – blockhouse. These classifications were merged in 1938 so that you had, for example, an artillery and MG half caponier – OPPK – *orudiyno-pulemetnyi polukaponir.*

Machine-gun shelters

Most of the shelters were designed for machine guns and each one had a similar set up. They tended to have two fighting compartments and two or three loopholes, an observation room with periscope, an entrance and gas lock. The entrance was covered by an internal loophole and an adjacent opening that allowed the blast from an explosive charge to dissipate. The positions were also fitted with standard equipment including air filtration systems, to protect against gas attacks, water storage tanks, electric generators and radio/telephone communications. Sleeping accommodation was not provided in the shelter so separate wooden shelters were constructed nearby.

The vast majority of the shelters in the Stalin and Molotov lines were armed with the 7.62mm M1910 Maxim machine gun. This was already dated and extremely heavy, but it was very reliable and capable of firing at 500–600 rounds a minute. It was water cooled and a system of pipes linked to a water tank prevented it from overheating. Further pipes vented the fumes from the gun outside. When firing the Maxim was also extremely noisy and made it difficult for the commander to issue orders through the traditional voice tube, so a fire control system using lights was introduced.

When used in a bunker the Maxim was fitted to a special carriage. The first design that was introduced was the metal Yushin carriage, but this proved to be too expensive and was redesigned by Kondakov (the famous gun designer) and bore his name (although confusingly it was also often referred to as the

BELOW
A photo montage depicting the NPS 3 machine-gun mount, which replaced the Gornostalev carriage for mounting the Maxim M1910 machine gun. This provided greater protection for the crew, especially when under attack. A telescopic sight mounted above the gun enabled the crew to aim the weapon. (S. Zaloga)

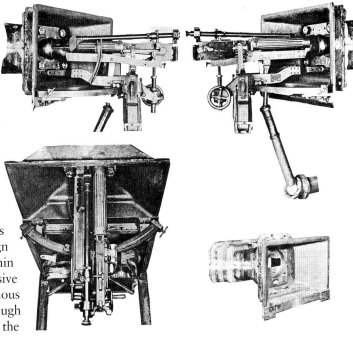

Yushin carriage). By far the most widely used carriage, however, was the Gornostalev carriage (named after the Chief of the Experimental Mechanical Laboratory). This was made from wood and although not the most effective it was simple and cheap to produce. Two versions of this carriage were produced: the P31 or P31a, which was a fixed version, and the PS31, which could be removed, enabling the crew to dismantle the machine gun and carriage and replace it with a telescope for observation.

The gun and the crew were protected from enemy fire by a hinged armoured flap. Early models suffered from a number of teething problems and it was only with the introduction of the P31 (Model 1931) that these were overcome. The P31 was the most widely used of the armoured flaps up until 1938, and could be closed, fully opened for firing or fixed half open for observation. To counter the threat from gas the embrasure could be sealed while still allowing the weapon to fire.

Despite the improvements to the MG carriage and armoured flap the solution was still far from ideal and a new, more elaborate housing was developed – the NPS-3. A forged armoured plate, which was recessed to minimize damage from ricochets, was fitted to an opening in the shelter. A ball mount was fitted to the armoured housing and this had two openings: one for the barrel of the Maxim machine gun and one for the telescopic sight used to aim the weapon.

To provide close-in fire support small openings were let into the side of the bunker. These were fitted with armoured plates that could accommodate the 7.62mm Degtyareva light machine gun. This example was in a bunker in the Przemysl Fortified Region of the Molotov Line. (Author's photograph)

Shelters were also armed with the 7.62mm DP (Pulemet Degtyareva Pekhotnii) machine gun. In the early pillboxes it was used to cover the entrance where a loophole was provided with an armoured flap that could be closed when not in use. Later, a special embrasure, the PZ-39, was developed to take the DT (Pulemet Degtyareva Tankovii) machine gun. This was designed for use in tanks and had a slightly larger drum and heavier barrel than the DP.

B MACHINE-GUN CASEMATE IN THE STALIN LINE

By far the most common weapon used in the fortifications of the Stalin and Molotov lines was the machine gun – either the 7.62mm Maxim Model 1910, which formed the main armament, or the 7.62mm Degtyareva which was generally used in a secondary role to cover the entrance. The Maxim was installed in a number of different ways and these became increasingly elaborate, going from a simple wooden mount with armoured flap to a special ball mount with integral sight.

The bunkers of the Stalin Line, as depicted here, were constructed in the 1930s and were generally of a simple design. Pillbox No. 139 was located near the village of Loshany and served as both a MG pillbox and command post for the commander of a company defence area in the Minsk Fortified Region. It was armed with three Maxim Model 1910 machine guns that covered an arc of more than 180 degrees. The machine guns were mounted on wooden Gornostalev carriages named after their designer. The carriage enabled the weapon to

be traversed 60 degrees and gave limited vertical movement (+/- 5 degrees). A simple armoured flap mounted on a pivot could be lowered when the weapon was not in use to protect the crew. The machine gun was fitted to a water cooling system and spent rounds were captured in a sack. The gunner was provided with a seat, as was his assistant.

The pillbox was entered by either of two steel gates at the rear (A and B) that could be covered by two Degtyareva machine guns from within the shelter. A series of gas locks led from the entrance to two fighting compartments. To the left was the larger of the two compartments that housed two Maxim machine guns and the observation room where a periscope was fitted into the ceiling. A door led from here to the other fighting compartment, which was fitted with a further Maxim MG. Because of its dual role as MG pillbox and command bunker it was also fitted with two '6PK type' radio sets and two field phones of 'UNA-I' and 'UNA-F' type.

B Machine-gun casemate in the Stalin Line

A

B

Plan view of gun emplacement

23

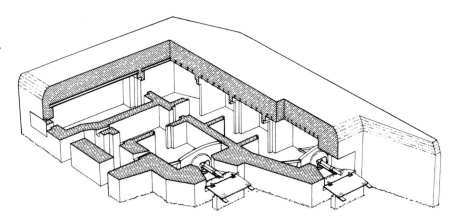

Drawing of a half-caponier bunker mounting two 76.2mm M1902 guns on M1932 mounts. In this example the armoured shields are lowered and the guns readied for action. When not in use the shields could be raised to protect the weapons. This type of shelter was used in the Stalin Line. (T. Idzikowski)

BELOW LEFT
A close-up view of a 76.2mm M1902 gun on M1932 mount, which formed the main armament of bunker No. 134 in the Minsk Fortified Region. The gun is fitted to an armoured shield, which is held in place by two steel bars on either side. Vision slits above the gun allowed the crew to see out. Just visible in the top right corner is one of the cranking handles for raising and lowering the protective armoured plate. (Author's photograph)

BELOW RIGHT
The embrasure of an artillery caponier in the Kamenets Podolski Fortified Region. The main 76.2mm gun in an L17 mount is still in place, and just above the barrell it is possible to see the opening for the gunner's sight. The gun was later removed by scrap metal merchants. (P. Netesov courtesy of E Hitriak and I Volkov)

Artillery bunkers

As well as shelters for machine guns, the Soviets also developed casemates to mount 76.2mm guns. They were generally mounted in two-storey reinforced concrete structures where the lower level housed the machinery, filtration units and ammunition and the upper level was where the fighting compartments were located. Two guns were normally fitted adjacent to each other, or one was slightly recessed behind the other and they were constructed as caponiers (with guns installed on both sides) or half caponiers (with guns on only one side). The positions were also provided with counter measures against infantry attack with a steel entrance door and internal doors, but once the enemy was close in, the fate of the bunker was invariably sealed.

Initially, the shelters housed the older M1900 or M1902 gun that was fitted to the Durliacher caponier mount and later the M1932 mount. Some of the early positions were open but later ones were fully enclosed. The guns were protected by a hinged armoured flap that was raised and lowered using a windlass. However, when the weapon was in use this arrangement afforded the crew little protection from small-arms fire and shell splinters and no protection against gas, so a new design was developed.

The result was essentially a scaled-up version of the ball-mounted machine gun mount for the Maxim and was known as the L17 mount. As with the machine-gun mount, a stepped armoured box was fitted into an embrasure set into the wall of the shelter. The ball mount was fitted inside and enabled the weapon to move freely laterally and horizontally. An aiming device allowed the operator to identify targets, although forward observers would

also be used. The weapon was fitted with a recoil mechanism and a system for ejecting used shell cases.

Anti-tank gun shelters

Shelters in the Stalin Line were only equipped with machine guns or artillery. However, the need to develop defences to counter the threat posed by the tank became increasingly apparent. As a result, a number of shelters were designed to mount a 45mm anti-tank gun (which at that time was more than capable of defeating any enemy armour) and were employed in the Molotov Line.

Just like the L17 mount for the 76.2mm gun and the NPS-3 mount for the Maxim, the 45mm AT gun was fitted in a ball mount in an armoured housing, which was again recessed to reduce damage from ricochets. The 45mm gun was mounted coaxially with a 7.62mm Degtyareva machine gun. The weapons were moved vertically and horizontally by means of hand wheels and were aimed through an offset telescope. The weapons were fired by a gunner seated to the side using a foot pedal and the spent rounds were ejected into a chute and then outside. Flexible exhaust tubes attached to the weapons ensured any noxious gases were expelled from the shelter.

This design was complicated and expensive, so a simpler and cheaper design was developed to house a split-trail 45mm gun that fired through an embrasure

BELOW RIGHT
The spent shells from the 76.2mm guns were ejected and passed through an opening in the floor to the fosse outside. The outside opening into the fosse is visible and in this case was fitted with an armoured flap (which is missing). On the ground is a shaped piece of concrete, which ensured that the spent shells were diverted away from the opening. (Author's photograph)

BELOW LEFT
The embrasure for a 45mm gun in the Kamenets Podolski Fortified Region. This position is somewhat unusual in that the original 45mm gun was, until recently, still in situ. It is now in a museum. The barrel is blocked by a shell. (P. Netesov courtesy of E Hitriak and I Volkov)

C **OVERLEAF: ARTILLERY CASEMATE FOR 76.2MM GUN**

A number of larger shelters in the Stalin and Molotov lines were fitted with 76.2mm guns. These were able to provide indirect fire and, as with this example which formed part of the Brest Fortified Region of the Molotov Line, were often built on two levels. The lower level (A) housed the crew's living quarters, together with the toilets and washroom (the water being drawn from a well), the filtration equipment and engine room and was also used to store munitons and other supplies. It was also the location of the emergency exit. The upper level (B) was home to the main entrance, which was protected by a series of gas locks and covered by a small loophole. (C) is a side view of the casemate showing both the upper and lower floors. Beyond the entrance was a stand-to area with access to the lower level and a door to

the observation room which was fitted with a periscope. From here the crew could gain access to both fighting compartments, one of which was additionally fitted with a loophole to cover the main access. Each fighting compartment was equipped with a 76.2mm gun on the more modern L17 mount.

The L17 mount was essentially a scaled-up version of the ball-mounted MG mount for the Maxim. An armoured box was set into an embrasure of the shelter. This recessed housing was stepped to reduce damage to the weapon as a result of ricochets. The ball mount was fitted inside and enabled the weapon to move freely vertically and horizontally. A telescopic sight allowed the operator to identify targets. The weapon was fitted with a recoil mechanism and a system for ejecting used shell cases.

Artillery casemate for 76.2mm gun (caption on previous page)

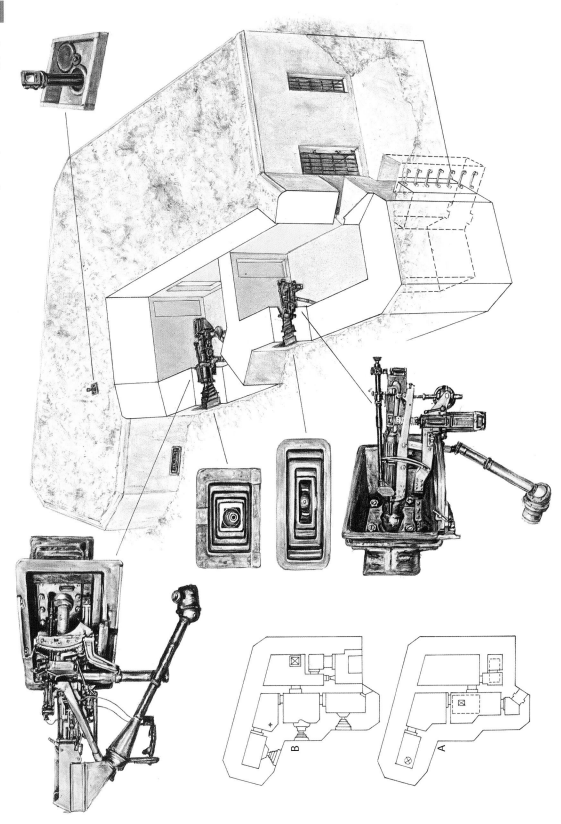

D

B

A

The vast majority of the bunkers built in the Stalin and Molotov lines housed machine guns. However, the need to develop defences to counter the threat posed by the tank became increasingly apparent. As a result a number of shelters were designed to mount a 45mm anti-tank gun (which at that time was more than capable of defeating any enemy armour).

The most elaborate of these were built in the Molotov Line, as in the case of this bunker, which formed part of the Brest Fortified Region. It was constructed over two levels. On the lower level (A) were the living quarters, filter room, store, engine room, wash room and toilet, emergency exit and well.

A vertical shaft with ladder linked the living quarters with the upper level of the shelter (B). As well as being home to the access shaft this room was linked via a door to the gas lock which led to the main entrance. The room also had a small loophole that allowed the crew to bring small-arms fire to bear on anyone trying to gain access to the shelter through the main door.

A further loophole in one of the fighting compartments housing a 7.62mm Maxim machine gun also enabled the crew to cover the entrance. From here a door led to the main fighting compartment. This is where the 45mm anti-tank gun was located. It was fitted in a ball mount in an armoured recessed housing that served to reduce damage from ricochets. A door at the rear led to the main entrance and the access shaft to the lower level. A further door led through from the main fighting compartment to the observation room. This in turn was linked to the final fighting compartment mounting another 7.62mm Maxim machine gun which could provide enfilade fire.

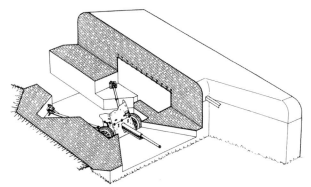

ABOVE LEFT
The increased need for anti-tank guns led to the development of a bunker to house the 45mm gun with split trail. The recess under the embrasure was for the wheels of the gun. The bunker was poorly finished with the wire reinforcing mesh still visible through the concrete. (Author's photograph)

ABOVE RIGHT
A drawing of a bunker mounting a Soviet 45mm gun, which was developed to meet the growing threat from tanks. The gun was an almost exact copy of the German 37mm PaK 35/36. This example formed part of the Molotov Line and was constructed near Przemysl in Poland. (T. Idzikowski)

Tank turrets

The more traditional fortifications of the Stalin and Molotov lines were supplemented by the addition of emplaced tank turrets or *Tankovaya ognievaya totshka* (TOT). Obsolete T18 tanks were sent to various fortified regions and a number were simply buried in the ground so that just the turret was visible. This made access difficult, so two further designs were developed with access through a hole in the base of the hull linked to a revetted tunnel that led to the rear. Some retained their main armament, others had their main gun removed and replaced with twin 7.62mm Degtyareva machine guns, and a number had their armament removed completely and were used as observation positions. A number of T24s were also sent to the fortified regions for use in this way, but seemingly many of the turrets (and those from T18s) sat in warehouses until the German invasion in 1941, by which time it was too late to install them.

Later a specially designed bunker was developed – the Type 'T' (Tank) pillbox – to mount obsolete T26 turrets. The bunker was divided into three sections. To the rear was the entrance. This was secured by a steel gate that could be covered by the radio operator firing through a small aperture. A corridor led to the 'technical room' that was secured with a steel-covered wooden door. The technical room housed a switchboard/telephone and a hand-operated ventilator. A further door led from the technical room to the fighting compartment directly underneath the turret. This was fitted with a ladder that linked the two and was also used to store extra ammunition.

The position was manned by five to six men who were housed in a dugout some 40m away. This, along with a further dugout for extra ammunition,

provisions and fuel, was linked to the shelter by a revetted trench. The whole position was extremely well camouflaged to compensate for the fact that it was vulnerable to enemy fire.

Mina

The Soviets built a number of *mina*, which were similar to the German *Werkgruppe* of the West Wall and the *Gros Ouvrages* of the Maginot Line. These consisted of a number of blocks armed with a mixture of machine guns and artillery, all linked by a series of tunnels (or posterns). The *mina* were relatively modest in scale when compared with their German and French counterparts that sometimes had narrow gauge railways, but they were nevertheless considerable feats of engineering. The tunnels had to be bored into the hillside and were sufficiently large to accommodate a man walking upright. Along their length there were often internal defence positions to counter enemy incursions should they gain access to the tunnel system. There was also a series of rooms that branched off the main tunnel network that had to be hewn out of the rock. These included storerooms, shower and toilet facilities, a communications room, boiler room and accommodation, although invariably not enough for the entire garrison.

ABOVE LEFT
The entrance to the underground gallery of a *mina* located near the village of Yurovka in the Kiev Fortified Region. The *mina* consisted of five machine-gun pillboxes linked by tunnels which are now flooded. The position was commanded by Lt Vetrov in the fighting of August 1941. (A. Kainaryan)

ABOVE RIGHT
This bunker was buit in the town of Novograd Volynski (Zwiahel) and formed part of a *mina* near Gulsk. The M1 pillbox was armed with three machine guns and covered the River Slucz. Just visible in the centre is the top of the observation tube. (A. Kainaryan)

Command and Observation Post No. 204 located near Yurovka village in the Kiev Fortified Region. This Type 'B' shelter was fitted with two GAU armoured cupolas. The one in the foreground has a number of gouges from enemy fire. Also just visible is the memorial to the men who died. (A. Kainaryan)

A T26 turret – a typical installation on the Stalin Line

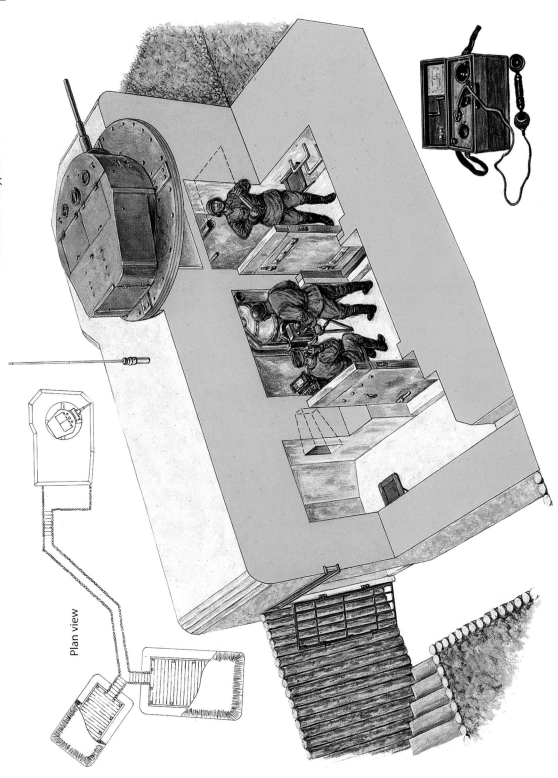

Plan view

The Soviet Union was the first country to use tank turrets as fixed fortifications, or *Tankovaya ognievaya totshka* (TOT). Initially, obsolete T18 and T24 tanks were simply buried in the ground so that just their turret was visible, but later T26 turrets were mounted on specially designed bunkers – the Type 'T' pillbox.

The turret sat above the fighting compartment where the ammunition was stored. This was secured with a steel covered wooden door which led to the 'technical room' that housed the radio, telephone and ventilator. A further door led from here to a short corridor and then to the main entrance which was protected by a further door and a steel bar gate covered by a loophole.

The position was normally manned by five men. There was a commander, loader and a further crew member who passed ammunition up into the turret. In addition there was a radio operator who was also responsible for covering the main entrance and someone to operate the ventilator. The tank turrets tended to be built just behind the main positions of the line and were often supported by other pillboxes. They were extremely well camouflaged to compensate for the fact that they were stationary targets and the turret armour was relatively thin.

Armoured turrets

Some bunkers in both the Stalin and Molotov lines were fitted with armoured cupolas, but the number was limited. There were two reasons for this. Firstly, the Izhorsk factory that manufactured them could not meet the demand as well as fulfilling the need for armoured shields for embrasures. Secondly, the cupolas were very expensive, and with severe budget constraints throughout the period little money could be spared for armoured turrets.

Nevertheless, a number of different turrets were produced. The GAU type was a modernized version of the turret developed by F. Golenkin before World War I. It was constructed in three parts – two semicircular halves and a roof. Often the top of the turret was fitted with an armoured belt for added protection. Access to the turret was through a hatch in the floor. Once inside the crew had all-round observation through four slits, each fitted with triplex glass.

The VSU observation cupola was rarely used on the western front, but rather on coastal fortifications. Like the GAU type it was constructed in three parts and had four observation slits. Two further variants of the VSU type were developed. The VSU turret for a single machine gun (or Butakov type) was of a similar design to the observation turret but was constructed from three armoured plates and a roof and was fitted with a Maxim machine gun on a central pedestal. This could be rotated to fire out of any of the four loopholes, which could be closed when not in use. The turret was generally mounted on M2-type bunkers. The VSU turret for two machine guns was larger again and was constructed from four steel plates and a roof section, and as a general rule was mounted on B-type bunkers.

Following the defeat of Poland the Soviets took ownership of the eastern fortifications constructed by the Poles in the inter-war period. Many of these

BELOW LEFT
Machine-gun pillbox No. 131 located near Kremenische village in the Kiev Fortified Region. This is a 'B' type shelter and is fitted with a Voenno-Stroitelnoe Upravlenie (VSU) armoured cupola with two MGs. The position was commanded by Lt Yakunin; in the fighting in July 1941 he was killed along with the rest of his men. (A. Kainaryan)

BELOW RIGHT
An armoured cupola fitted to an artillery half-caponier bunker in the Przemysl Fortified Region. Many of these were stripped from Polish forts seized by the Soviets in 1939. The turrets were set into larger holes and then concreted into place as can be seen here. This bunker covered the River San. (Author's photograph)

The inside view of one of the Glavnoye Artilleriyskoe Upravlenie (GAU) armoured cupolas. The cupola was reached via a steel rung ladder that led to an armoured door, which could be secured from the inside. (A. Kainaryan)

were fitted with armoured turrets that were much admired by Soviet engineers and a decision was taken to remove them and fit them to the new defences of the Molotov Line.

Passive defences

In addition to the concrete pillboxes and bunkers, passive defences were constructed to counter the threat from tanks and infantry. Anti-tank ditches were dug at the forward edge of the fortified region. These were revetted with wood to provide added strength and were dug in a zigzag pattern. Elsewhere 'dragon's teeth' or steel hedgehogs were used, as were steel girders or wooden piles rammed into the ground at an angle. As a last resort boulders were used as an improvised anti-tank defence. The main defensive positions were also protected by barbed wire and mines, although mines were not extensively used as they only tended to be laid during mobilization, and the surprise German attack gave engineers little time to lay them.

THE LIVING SITES

As with so many defences constructed in the inter-war period, the fortifications of the Stalin and Molotov lines were not designed for permanent occupation. However, from 1928 through to the spring of 1941 the border area was alive with engineers, labourers and soldiers as they worked to complete firstly the Stalin Line and then the defences along the new border. Initially the construction plan was modest with work on only four fortified regions but eventually it grew to ten times that number with a corresponding increase in workers, overseers and supporting units. Once complete these defences were to be manned by specially trained fortress troops whose job it was to slow the enemy advance and allow the reserves to mobilize. Tragically for millions of Russian soldiers, many of the fortifications were not ready for combat when Hitler launched Operation *Barbarossa* and the troops manning the defences were unable to significantly slow the German advance, leaving the Red Army, still readying itself to fight, exposed to the full force of the German *blitzkrieg*.

A set of concrete dragon's teeth in the Przemysl Fortified Region, which were used by the Soviets as anti-tank obstacles. In this case they were constructed in front of a bunker mounting a 45mm anti-tank gun to provide the ideal killing ground. (Author's photograph)

Construction work on the Stalin Line

In the summer and autumn of 1927 preparatory work began on the first four fortified regions of the Stalin Line. To supervise the work a special committee was convened, the Komitet po Injenernoi Podgoptovke Teatrov Voennyh Dejstvii (Committee for the Engineering Preparation of the Theatres of Military Action), and its terms of reference were outlined by K.E. Voroshilov, the People's Commissar for Military and Naval Affairs (Narkom-Voenmor), in November 1927. The committee was responsible for overseeing the progress of the building work, but not for producing guidance on the design and construction of the fortifications. That job rested with the Military Construction Directorate (Voenno-Stroitelnoe Upravleniia, or VSU RKKA) and more specifically with the Second Department, or Department for the Construction of Permanent Defensive Installations (Otdel Stroitelstva Kapitalnyh Oboronitelnyh Soorujenii), under the auspices of G.M. Golembatovskii. This guidance covered not only the construction of the fortifications, but also detailed how civil authorities and citizens in the fortified regions should co-ordinate their economic activities to expedite the building work. This even went so far as to stipulate the requirement to supply the sites with fodder for the horses provided by local peasants to move goods.

The entranceway to a bunker in the Polotsk Fortified Region. These were constructed in 1930 when there was less pressure to complete the work and unusually the builders have taken the time to include a Soviet star above the door. Also just visible are the impressions from the shuttering boards and the internal loophole. (Author's photograph)

In 1932 responsibility for the fortifications programme was reorganized. Already in 1931 the Special Inspectorate of Engineering Troops (Specialnaya Inspekciya Inzhenernykh Voysk) had started to assume control in place of the Military Construction Directorate and now a decision was taken to combine the Special Inspectorate of Engineering Troops and the Second Department of the Military Construction Directorate and create the Directorate of Chief Engineers of the Military Construction Directorate of the Red Army (Upravleniia Nachal'nika Ingenerov Voenno-stroitelnogo Upravleniia – UNI VSU RKKA). This organization was now responsible for all organizational and technical issues in respect of the fortifications programme.

F   **OVERLEAF: DETAILED VIEW OF THE FORTIFIED POSITION OF ZWIAHEL**

As part of the Stalin Line the Soviets constructed a number of forts or *mina*. Two of these were built on the River Slucz: one at Novograd-Volynski (Zwiahel) and one near the village of Gulsk (Hulsk) – known to the Germans as Werkgruppe A and Werkgruppe B respectively. The fort at Novograd-Volynski, shown here, was built into a small hill overlooking the river and consisted of a series of machine gun and artillery blocks that were linked together via a series of tunnels. In total there were six blocks. Block 101 (1) was located on the forward slope as was Block 102 (2), but set further up. Both were fitted with three Maxim machine guns that covered the western approaches across the river. Block 100 (3) to the north and Block 104 (4) to the south were each fitted with two Maxim MGs and covered the flanks. These blocks were reached by vertical shafts which linked the fighting compartment to the main tunnel system. As well as the fighting compartments

these blocks had ammunition stores, ventilation plants, latrines and emergency exits.

To the rear of the position was Block 103 (5), a half-caponier (which meant it fired to only one side), which was fitted with two Model 1902 76.2mm guns. These were positioned to cover any enemy assault from the south. The block itself was slightly more elaborate than the others in the fort. It had its own entrance, but was also linked to the main tunnel system by a shaft which was fitted with a hoist to move ammunition. The guns were mounted in separate fighting compartments and were equipped with spent cartridge recesses under the floor. A separate ammunition room was provided which was fitted with a loophole to cover the entrance. A final block, Block 99 (not shown), was somewhat unusual in that it was not linked to the main fort by a tunnel. It was located to the north-east of the position and provided some protection to the entrance (6).

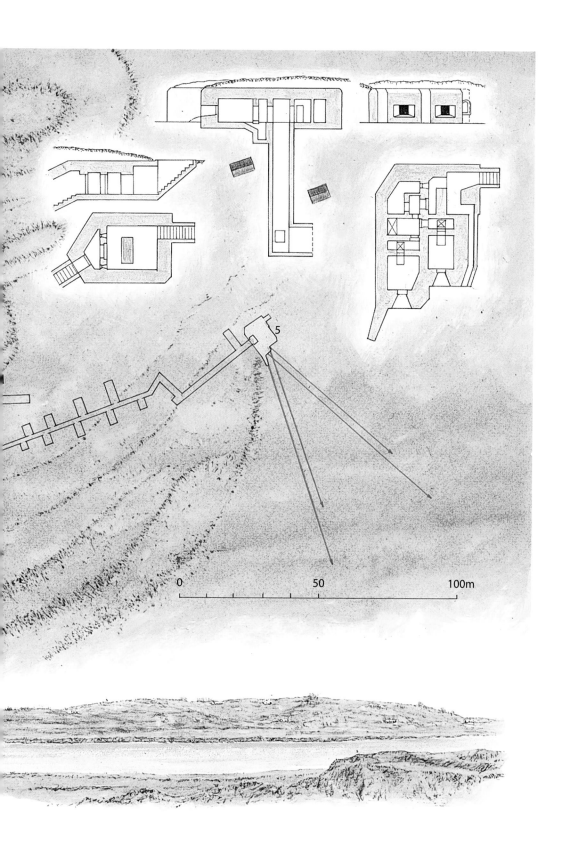

5

0   50   100m

The sheer scale and complexity of the construction programme meant that it was necessary to enlist the help of other departments. The Scientific Proving Ground of the Artillery Directorate (Nauchnoispytatelnyi Orujeinyi Polygon Artilleriiskogo Upravleniia or NIOP AU US RKKA) developed the armoured embrasure covers and sealing units, and the permanent and temporary machine-gun mounts as well as the elaborate machine-gun cooling system. The Military Chemical Directorate (Voenno-Himicheskoe Upravleniia or VoHimU) and the Military Technical Directorate (Voenno-Tehnicheskoe Upravleniia or VTU) collaborated on the development of the filter and ventilation equipment, while other directorates worked on the electrification of the shelters and their camouflage.

Responsibility for the building work itself fell under the auspices of the Military Labour Directorate (Upravleniia Nachal'nika Voennostroitel'nyh, or UNVSR), which had been formed in 1924–25 to oversee all military building projects. This was a small department with only 32 staff, but they had a wealth of experience of concrete construction.

With the rapid expansion in the building programme in the early 1930s the UNVSR was also reorganized with the creation of individual labour directorates – *upravleniia nachal'nika rabot*, or UNR. Each UNR was subordinated to the Military Construction Directorate, but was directly responsible for the day-to-day control of the work in individual fortified regions. The UNR could assign labour and could also call on engineers and troops in the region to help with the construction work.

Each UNR was broken down into *uchastki*, which were administrative sectors or sites that were responsible for the construction of bunkers in a particular area of the fortified region. Broadly speaking, each *uchastki* was responsible for one battalion defence region and was generally responsible for the construction of ten positions, although where the site was more dispersed it may have only been five to seven. However, often 20 or more positions were planned for a battalion defence region; this put a strain on the workers and as a result quality suffered. *Poduchastki* or subsectors/sites were responsible for company defence regions.

The process for establishing a fortified region, as would be expected in a planned economy, was somewhat convoluted. The Defence Committee (Komitet Oborony) made the initial recommendation for the establishment of the fortified region and the Revolutionary Military Soviet (Revvoensoviet, RVS) endorsed the decision with the issue of a special decree or *postanovleie*. The headquarters of the military district (where the fortified region was to be constructed) then outlined a plan of construction for BDRs and CDRs and this was approved by the Revvoensoviet, which also appointed the head of the UNR and outlined the terms of reference for the reconnoitring of the fortified region. The positions were reconnoitred and the findings endorsed by the Military District and the Revvoensoviet. The final scheme was laid down in the general plan of construction in the fortified region. With the plan finalized the UNR organized and assigned plans of work.

The construction work was conducted in four phases. Firstly, the preparatory work was completed, which involved the site survey, the stockpiling of raw materials and the construction of the accommodation for the workers. Secondly, the ground was prepared, which necessitated digging trenches, putting in place the reinforcing rods, constructing the shuttering and making arrangements to produce the concrete. Thirdly, the concrete was mixed and poured. Finally, the shuttering was removed, drainage work was completed and the equipment was fitted. With the work complete the fields of fire were cleared and the bunker camouflaged.

Construction of the Molotov Line

Following the partition of Poland a decision was taken to fortify the new border. Little progress was made during the winter of 1939/40 due in no small part to the poor weather. The following spring, news of the defeat of France gave the work an added urgency. With the ink still drying on the peace signed by the French, Marshal Timoshenko issued an order for work to start on the border defences. This marked the true beginning of the construction of the Molotov Line, with work commencing on 11 new fortified regions from Finland in the north, along the border with East Prussia and down into what had been Poland.

The work was co-ordinated by the Directorate of Defensive Construction (Upravleniia Oboronitel'nogo Stroitel'stva), which formed part of General Khrenov's Main Military Engineering Directorate with technical assistance provided by officers within the General Staff. It was soon realized, however, that limited resources meant it would be impossible to run two building programmes in parallel so work on all but one of the eight fortified regions of the Stalin Line that was still progressing was suspended. Workers were now transferred to the west, including 84 construction battalions, 25 construction companies and 25 motor transport battalions as well as an indeterminate number of civilian workers.

This change of priority came as a surprise to some. Sandalov, Chief of the Operations Department in the headquarters of the Kiev Special MD, only found out that work had stopped on the defences when he visited the Slutsk Fortified Region. All the construction units in the region, together with the district engineer regiment and several engineer battalions were now reallocated to the area around the old fortress town of Brest.

Even with this additional manpower, progress on the new defences was slow, and in the spring of 1941 Khrenov was dismissed. Responsibility for the fortifications now passed from the Military Engineering Directorate to a separate directorate under the command of Marshal Shaposhnikov. At the same time work began on a further seven fortified regions and surveys were completed at three possible sites along the new border with Romania. This meant that, 'The number of fortified areas simultaneously under construction by spring 1941 was equal to the entire number built or begun in the western Soviet Union from the late 1920s through 1939' (Tarleton, 1993, p.43).

The expanded construction programme placed an even greater strain on resources. The need for additional manpower was relatively easily satisfied with more workers sent to the border zone, so that by the spring of 1941 nearly 136,000 men were working on the defences (58,000 in the Baltic, 35,000 in the Western and 43,000 men in the Kiev military districts). A further 160 engineer battalions from the border districts and 41 engineer battalions from elsewhere were also ordered to help. But this increase in manpower did nothing to overcome the inability of Soviet industry to produce the necessary concrete and steel or to manufacture armaments and equipment for the pillboxes. The possibility of raising production levels was discussed, but it was soon realized that this was impossible. The only solution was to strip equipment from the Stalin Line, but this was far from satisfactory, not least because much of it was unsuitable for the new emplacements.

To make matters worse, the fortification programme was not alone in placing demands on these scarce resources. Men and materials were needed to build new airfields, railways and roads as well as barrack blocks and warehouses. And of course the men, machines and materials needed to be moved to the border zone and there was a crippling shortage of transport vehicles, so much so that trucks and tractors from artillery units were pressed into use.

The partially completed escape shaft of a half-caponier in the Minsk Fortified Region. The exposed reinforcing rods would have been used to secure the remaining section of the shaft. Somewhat unusually, the original wooden shuttering remains to this day. (V. Tadra)

All of these factors combined meant that by the time of the German invasion only 2,500 positions had been completed, and of these fewer than a thousand were fully equipped.

The workers

Following the decision in 1927 to establish four fortified regions, the Red Army created a number of specialized construction units. These were often manned by raw conscripts who were considered to lack the wherewithal for service in regular units and as such were well suited to this work. The modest scale of the undertaking meant that it was relatively straightforward to meet the initial manpower requirement. However, the expansion of the construction programme from 1930 onwards and the establishment of additional construction units placed a greater strain on resources and the ranks were combed once again for possible recruits; now, seemingly, even prisoners were sent to work on the defences. But even such desperate measures failed to meet the requirement and it proved necessary to hire civil labourers. Local peasants were also used, often to transport building materials. Indeed those living in or near a fortified region were obliged to work a certain number of hours on the defences.

The army conscripts who were sent to the construction units would spend three months at a building site before being relieved. This cycle continued for nine months from the spring through to the autumn, when work was suspended because of the severe winter weather. However, delays due to the lack of materials meant that work often continued into the winter months. This worsened an already difficult job for the men of the construction units. The work was physically hard, the conditions were difficult and the pay was poor. Although Soviet propaganda tried to portray otherwise, the workers were not inspired by the revolutionary zeal of their leaders. These factors, combined with the shortages of raw materials, meant that the quality of the work suffered.

The decision to build a new line of defences along the revised border placed an even greater strain on manpower and meant that engineer troops were sent to work finishing off the permanent defences and constructing field fortifications. Some rifle units of the first echelon were also seconded. One battalion from each regiment on a rotating basis was ordered to spend a month at a time on construction work. Even with this additional manpower there was still much to do and so the local population was conscripted to complete unskilled work. Immediately before the German invasion 'Major General V.F Zotov, chief of the Baltic military engineers, had begun to call out the civilian population to dig trenches and positions in the frontier areas' (Erickson 2003, p.102).

The construction work continued until the very last minute in a desperate attempt to complete preparations and many of those working on the new border defences were caught up in the initial fighting. The war diary of 28th Rifle Corps records: 'like thunder from a clear sky, throughout the depth of the frontier zone, unexpectedly, the roar of a barrage. The surprise Fascist artillery-fire burst on those points where the rifle and engineer units building fortifications were spending the night' (Erickson 2003, p.118). On another occasion Lt. Gen. V.I. Boldin, deputy to Col. Gen. D.G. Pavlov, commander of the Western Front, on his way to assess the situation after the invasion, stopped a group of workers heading to the rear. He asked who they were and they replied that 'we have been working on the fortifications. But the place where we worked is now like a sea of flames.'

The engineers

As a general rule military engineers were in charge of each *uchastki*. One such was Pyotr Grigorenko, later a general in the Red Army, who served part of his apprenticeship training to become a military engineer working on the defences of the Mogilev–Podolski UR and later the Minsk UR. What he found shocked him. Workers would march to the construction site, but if that was some distance from their barracks they often did little more than rest and then march back to their quarters. If the construction site was closer then some work was completed, but it was far from satisfactory. Grigorenko found that 'not a single piece of equipment worked properly; doors would not close, fittings had rusted over, and the rooms in the emplacements were unsuitable even for use as vegetable storehouses' (Tarleton, 1992, p.195).

Grigorenko's experience was typical of many engineer officers, but as a junior officer he escaped the worst excesses of Stalin's purges. The Inspector, later Chief of Engineers, General Nikolai Petin was not so lucky, and was killed in 1937 in spite of the fact that he was awarded the Order of Lenin in recognition of the sterling work he had completed on the defences. The vicious purge of the officer class had a particularly damaging effect on the cadre of engineers and meant that military students, or more often civilian engineers, had to be employed to oversee the work. These civilians were perfectly competent at directing the construction work, but they had neither tactical awareness nor an understanding of how the military equipment should be fitted. Therefore, rather than make a mistake and be accused of sabotage they often did not complete the work, leaving them open to the lesser charge of laziness.

Manning the defences

The fortified regions

Somewhat confusingly the units that manned the defences were also called fortified regions, or *ukreplinnyje rajony*. The first of these units was established in 1923, but it was not until work on the Stalin Line began in earnest that the number increased significantly. Each fortified region was given a unit number and attached to an army. As a broad rule of thumb each of these units was allocated to a certain fortified region (Pskov, Kiev etc.), but larger or more important areas might be strengthened with the addition of other fortified regions (see Appendix A). The initial 13 fortified regions were manned by one or two machine-gun battalions, 25 in total, with 18,000 men under arms. Supporting the fortified regions were a number of artillery platoons and numerous ancillary units. In 1938 the number of fortified regions was increased from 13 to 21 and the number of troops grew proportionally.

Considering the length of the front that these units covered, the number of troops was relatively modest. Part of the reason for this was that they would be fighting in prepared positions and had at their disposal tremendous firepower with a mixture

Many of the bunkers of the Molotov Line were built in extreme haste, as in the case of this position in the Przemysl Fortified Region. Access to the basement where much of the heavy machinery was located was through a hatch, but here the ladder has been fitted in the wrong place, making entry almost impossible. (Author's photograph)

Some of the bunkers were fitted with rudimentary sanitary facilities for the crew. This example has two marks for the soldier to place his feet. The hatch to the side would have been covered. (Author's photograph)

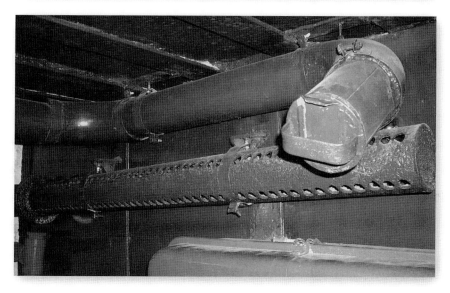

Fumes from the generator room were extracted through a pierced pipe and vented outside the shelter. However, the system was not found to be particularly effective and was later changed. (Author's photograph)

of artillery and machine guns. Moreover, the numbers represented the peacetime complement. In time of war the fighting strength of the fortified region would quadruple to 4,000 men with machine-gun and artillery companies brought up to battalion strength and the addition of auxiliary units.

In May 1941 as the spectre of war grew the People's Commissariat of Defence (NKO) ordered the fortified regions to be put on a war footing and mandated that each one be brought up to its full wartime complement. The mobilization was to be complete by 1 July for the western border defences and by 1 October for the old defences of the Stalin Line. In addition, this force was to be bolstered with a further 17 new fortified regions, which together with other units, would see the number of men swell by more than 120,000. However, the reinforcement plan did not start until the beginning of June and was nowhere near complete when the Germans invaded on 22 June 1941. On this fateful day the overall strength of the fortified regions, the majority of which (42 out of 57) were stationed in the west (with the remainder in the Far East), totalled 192,240. These troops were equipped with 1,700 guns and 9,800 light and heavy machine guns. But the impressive numbers could not disguise the fact that the fortified regions were not combat ready with only a third of officers and NCOs and less than half of regular troops manning the defences which themselves were only partially complete.

The NKVD

As well as the fortified regions, the border was manned by men of Beria's NKVD. These border guards were lightly armed and were charged with patrolling the frontier to detain transgressors and to counter the threat from insurgents. On paper the border guards represented a relatively significant force, with 49 NKVD detachments each with a strength of 1,400 to 2,000 men. However, they were not equipped or trained to repel an attack by regular forces, but they were able to provide early warning of an enemy attack and hold the line while the army mobilized and the infantry were brought forward to relieve them. That was the theory. In practice the rifle divisions were often held well to the rear and the speed of the German advance meant that they could not be mobilized in time (the first echelon was drawn back as far as 40km and the second echelon 100km).

OPERATIONAL HISTORY

In September 1939 Germany invaded Poland, and in four short weeks defeated the brave but hopelessly outdated Polish Army. With victory secured the spoils were shared between the victors in accordance with the Nazi–Soviet Non Aggression Pact of August 1939. After a brief respite Hitler turned his attention west and ordered his forces to attack France, the Low Countries, Denmark and Norway. He also planned to invade Britain, but the landings were delayed and then cancelled because of the failure of Göring's Luftwaffe to defeat the RAF in what became known as the Battle of Britain. His plan thwarted, Hitler once again looked east, where lay the possibility of destroying the birthplace of Bolshevism and securing *lebensraum* (living space) for the German people.

G | **GERMAN TACTICS FOR ATTACKING FORTIFIED POSITIONS**

The advance of Army Group South was met with well-coordinated and determined resistance and as a result the advance was steady rather than spectacular. It was not until the middle of July that the 22nd and 76th infantry divisions of 11th Army reached the River Dniester (Dnestr) and the fortifications of the Mogilev-Podolski Fortified Region. On 17 July they crossed the river, but unbeknownst to them they had bypassed an enemy strongpoint on the east bank. This had remained silent while the lead elements crossed the river, but now the four 76.2mm guns and a machine gun took their toll on the rear echelons.

Company B of 744th Engineer Regiment was now ordered to silence the position. The company, commanded by Leutnant Sander, crossed the river without incident and reconnoitred the position in order to pinpoint the embrasures and entrance. Once identified, a plan of action was formulated. The attacking force was divided into three squads. (1) The 1st Squad, led by Sander, advanced on the position from the rear and following a burst of flame from a flame thrower his squad destroyed the two guns on the left of the shelter with Bangalore torpedoes.

Now the 2nd Squad attacked the embrasures on the right side of the bunker. Explosives were used to remove the steel shutters and Bangalore torpedoes again used to silence the guns. Meantime the 3rd Squad had silenced the machine gun with a mixture of flamethrowers and grenades. (2) The 1st Squad now prepared to storm the bunker through the main entrance. The door was blasted open but the two soldiers who entered the bunker were killed by machine-gun fire. Later a second assault was launched. Flamethrowers silenced the enemy just long enough to allow explosive charges to be inserted in the entranceway. After these had detonated and the smoke cleared Sander entered the bunker with two men. The entrance was clear but a little way inside the corridor kinked left and when the three negotiated this turn Sander's men were hit and one killed. (3) With losses mounting it was decided to demolish the shelter rather than storm it and lose more lives. Two separate 550lb charges were placed against the outside walls and detonated. When the bunker was inspected in the morning the crew were all dead as a result of the fighting the previous day, the demolition charge or through suffocation.

German tactics for attacking fortified positions

German positions
Russian positions
German movements
Russian movements
Fields of fire
Route of engineer units

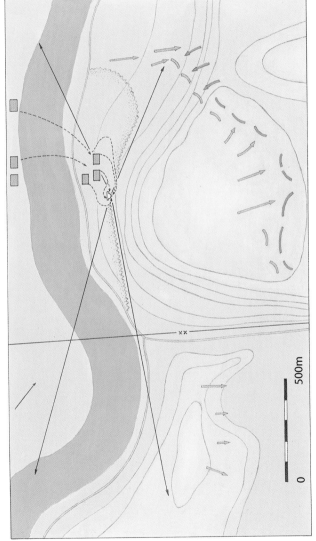

1

2

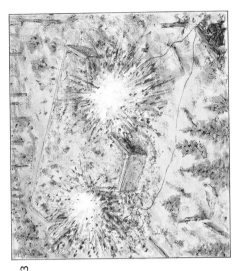

3

0 500m

A bunker of the Molotov Line located at Przemysl. The two embrasures have received direct hits from German guns in the fierce fighting to break through the defences in June 1941. The shuttering was erected to disguise the bunker and the steps at the side were constructed by the Germans. (T. Idzikowski)

On 22 June 1941 Hitler and his cohorts launched Operation *Barbarossa*, the invasion of the Soviet Union. On that momentous day some 3.6 million soldiers supported by 3,600 tanks and 2,700 aircraft crossed into Soviet-occupied Poland. This force, the largest in European military history, was split into three army groups each directed against a specific target – Moscow, Leningrad and Kiev – with the aim of destroying the Red Army. Ranged against the Axis armies were 2.9 million men, 10,000–15,000 tanks and 8,000 aircraft, which on paper at least seemed more than a match for Hitler's all-conquering Wehrmacht. However, much of the Soviet equipment was obsolete (with notable exceptions, like the T34, arguably the best medium tank of the war) and Stalin's purges in the 1930s had decimated the officer corps. In spite of these handicaps, the Red Army valiantly resisted the onslaught, but it proved no match for the German blitzkrieg and in a series of huge encirclements the Germans crushed the Soviet forces of the western military districts. Hitler's assertion that 'We have only to kick in the door and the whole rotten edifice will come crashing down' seemed to be coming true. By July Army Group North under Field Marshal von Leeb had all but cut off Leningrad. By October Army Group Centre, commanded by Field Marshal von Bock, was within striking distance of Moscow, and by the end of November lead elements were only 20km from the capital. On Bock's right flank Army Group South, under Field Marshal von Rundstedt, made similarly spectacular advances, and by the middle of September Kiev had been encircled.

From this evidence the casual observer might conclude that the defences of the Molotov and Stalin lines did little to stem the German advance, and broadly speaking this is the case. The defences of the Molotov Line had been hastily constructed along the new border with Germany, and when Hitler's surprise attack was launched they were neither complete nor fully manned. As one eminent historian concluded, 'Along almost the entire length of the vast front the German Army achieved tactical surprise … The field fortifications, either incomplete or unmanned, were quickly pierced by German troops' (Erickson, 2001, p.587). A similar fate befell many of the fortifications of the Stalin Line, which had been largely abandoned after Poland had been annexed. However, such generalizations obscure the fact that there were a number of fierce battles as German forces fought their way through the new and old border defences.

The Molotov Line

Army Group North

The attack on Leningrad by Army Group North was spearheaded by General Hoepner's 4th Panzer Army, comprising three Panzer divisions (1st, 6th and 8th) – supported by the 3rd and 36th Motorized divisions. These well-equipped and highly motivated units, all veterans of the Polish campaign and the fighting in the west (albeit often under different names), were ranged against determined, but poorly armed elements of Beria's NKVD. In spite of detailed intelligence indicating an imminent invasion, ten border guard detachments, rather than the specially trained fortification troops (*ukreplinnyje rajony*), manned the incomplete defences of the Molotov Line in the Baltic Special MD, with many regular units not at the front proper but still in camp (only on 21 June 1941 had Timoshenko ordered commanders of the military districts to man the defences of the fortified regions). And the ill-preparedness was exacerbated by the order to Col. Gen. F. Kuznetsov to 'do nothing, and do not provoke the Germans'.

Yet in spite of all the handicaps and the lack of leadership, there were a number of instances where units manning the defences put up determined resistance. For example, 1st Panzer Division was involved in a number of hard-fought skirmishes on 22 June. This was especially true of the fighting around Tauroggen and the fighting for the River Jura, where the lead elements of the division had to negotiate minefields and overcome pillboxes protected by barbed wire. At the same time 6th Panzer Division crossed the border near Tilsit; 'From the first day the resistance was somewhat stiffer than had been expected with Soviet border defences fighting stubbornly, and the Panzer IVs running out of ammunition before noon for the first time' (Ritgen, 1988, p.17) The resistance was short lived, however, and by the end of the first day's fighting the two divisions had made significant gains and 8th Panzer Division was almost off the map.

Although the armoured spearheads made the major inroads and enjoyed much of the credit for the early victories, the infantry still formed the mainstay of the German armies that attacked the Soviet Union. One such unit was the 12th Infantry Division, also a veteran of the Polish and French

An emplaced T18 tank with 45mm gun is inspected by SS troops in the distinctive splinter pattern fatigues. Camouflage that would have disguised the position lies strewn around. This turret was installed in the Stalin Line and was captured in the summer of 1941. (J. Magnuski courtesy of S. Zaloga)

A bunker of the Brest Fortified Region, which has two loopholes, one for a 45mm anti-tank gun on the left and one for a Maxim machine gun on the right. The front of the position is heavily pock marked from small-arms fire and a larger impact above the MG loophole. (Author's photograph)

campaigns, which now formed part of Busch's 16th Army advancing on 4th Panzer Army's southern flank. The maps the division received prior to the attack included little detail of what lay ahead, but from its advanced positions forward observers had been able to establish the nature and strength of the positions on its immediate front. In spite of this intelligence, the first hours of the attack were not easy. Around the village of Kunigiskiai, in Lithuania, the Soviets had built a series of bunkers supported by other outposts. These were tenaciously defended and repulsed the frontal assault of 3rd Battalion. It was not until 1st Battalion, advancing on its flank, had broken through the defences and entered the village from the rear, so cutting off the defenders' line of retreat, that the resistance finally ended. With this hurdle safely negotiated, the advance gathered pace and by the beginning of July the division had crossed the old Soviet frontier, which brought it up against the defences of the Stalin Line. This would be the division's next and sternest test.

Army Group Centre
The bulk of the panzers employed in Operation *Barbarossa* were concentrated in Army Group Centre under Bock. He planned to use the armour in a massive pincer movement with 3rd Panzer Army to the north and 2nd Panzer Army to the south. The enemy forces around Bialystok would be encircled and destroyed, much as Zhukov had demonstrated in the war game of January 1941.

General Hoth's 3rd Panzer Army was led by 20th and 7th Panzer divisions, which headed towards Alytus, and 12th Panzer Division, which advanced on Merkine on the River Neman. In spite of months of preparation, the lead units knew little if anything of the defences that faced them, but this seemed to be little handicap as the armoured fist smashed through the Molotov Line on 22 June and advanced on their respective objectives. In fact the difficult ground conditions proved more of an obstacle than the defences.

The 2nd Panzer Army, under the command of the mercurial Heinz Guderian, which formed the southern pincer, enjoyed similar success. Guderian was a great advocate of armour and planned to use his panzer divisions in two spearheads – 17th and 18th to the north of Brest and 3rd and 4th to the south. The attack met little resistance from troops manning the defences, and communication problems, endemic in Pavlov's sector of the front, added to the general confusion, as did the fact that the front was one big construction site: work was still continuing on the defences, and only at 0300 hours on 22 June 1941 did Pavlov order the fortified regions to be fully manned.

The two Panzer Armies were flanked to the north by Strauss's 9th Army and to the south by Kluge's 4th Army. These were principally made up of infantry divisions. One such was 28th Infantry Division, which formed part of 9th Army. Like Hoth's panzers, the two lead regiments were similarly untroubled by the defences, but the division's reserve regiment was not so lucky. Indeed, the reserve regiment's first experience came even before it had been committed when a company commander, Colonel Dr Alfred Durrwanger, was sent forward to establish the position of the lead units, which had been out of contact with headquarters for some time. Travelling on a motorcycle, Durrwanger reached the front and was almost immediately met with a hail of enemy fire from a bunker not marked on German maps (indeed, as he noted, most were not). He escaped unscathed and was able to report back to headquarters. Soon thereafter his regiment advanced, but the portion of the line they attacked was manned by 56th Rifle Division and 68th Fortified Region. These units 'defended a line of bunkers and fortifications, partly incomplete, but protected by trenches, with utmost tenacity … The Soviets had just occupied this line some days before and when attacked they had not retreated. They were very brave soldiers' (Glantz, 2004, p.235). Durrwanger's regiment took three days to overcome the defences and suffered heavy casualties, with 25 soldiers dead and 125 wounded.

Army Group South
For Rundstedt, the battle for the Molotov Line was far more challenging: 'Army Group South had to grind its way through solid Soviet defences manned by troops skilfully led and determined to fight' (Erickson, 2003, p.163). Unlike his compatriots Pavlov and Kuznetsov, Colonel-General Kirponos was able to man the defences along the border. The Vladimir-Volynski, Strumilov and Rava-Russkaia fortified areas, for example, were manned by men of 2nd, 4th and 6th fortified regions respectively and regular army units were mobilized and ordered to the front.

A bunker of the Molotov Line armed with two 76.2mm guns. Clearly visible are the armoured housings, which were stepped to reduce the damage from richochets. The iron framework protruding from the top of the bunker would have been used to secure camouflage. (T. Idzikowski)

Two German soldiers stand atop a captured bunker of the Molotov Line. The embrasures were damaged in the fighting to break through the Przemysl Fortified Region. Just visible between the two soldiers is the top of the armoured cupola. (T. Idzikowski)

Kleist's 1st Panzer Army was tasked with spearheading the attack. Under his command were three Panzer corps supported by regular infantry, and it was the latter that struggled to breach the enemy defences. 'The Silesians of the 298th and the Ostmark troops of the 44th Infantry Division in the first two days penetrate the tenaciously defended enemy fortifications in a bold assault' (Glantz, 2004, p.309). Once again, though, the Panzer divisions looked to seize the initiative. By probing the defences and identifying weaknesses, the Panzers looked to outflank the defences and break into the rear. The most ominous pressure was exerted in the gap between the Vladimir-Volynski and Strumilov fortified regions, which also broadly coincided with the junction of the Soviet 5th and 6th armies. Having broken through the defences, 1st Panzer Army and Reichenau's 6th Army drove a wedge 50km wide between the two Soviet armies.

To the south, Stulpnagel's 17th Army also looked to exploit the element of surprise in its battle for the Rava-Russkaia and Przemysl fortified regions, but again Kirponos had time to mobilize his troops and man the defences. These troops were able to inflict a series of reverses on the enemy. The 41st Rifle Division and 91st Border Guard Detachment defending the Rava-Russkaia Fortified Region met the onslaught of three infantry divisions and elements of a Panzer division of 17th Army and repelled the assaults for five days; the garrison of the Przemysl Fortified Region did not surrender its position for seven days. But despite these heroics, Kirponos was unable to hold the line and by 24 June 17th Army had opened up a fissure some 30km wide. Kirponos was now forced to order 6th and 26th armies to abandon their positions in the Rava-Russkaia and Przemysl fortified regions and fall back towards Lwów (Lemberg).

With a few exceptions the defences of the Molotov Line 'though tenaciously defended ... were reduced or bypassed on the first day of the war' (Tarleton, 1993, p.51). The Red Army now fell back in disarray towards the Stalin Line. Those troops seeking salvation in the old fortifications were in for a nasty surprise.

The Stalin Line

Army Group North

With the border defences now far behind them, Leeb's army group continued its advance towards Leningrad. Once again Hoepner's Panzers were in the van and by the end of June the lead elements had reached the Western Dvina. Timoshenko was determined to hold this line and on 25 June he ordered Colonel-General Kuznetsov to organize a 'stubborn defence' of the river; however, the horse had already bolted. On 26 June 56th Panzer Corps reached the Western Dvina and both 8th Panzer and 3rd Motorized divisions soon established a bridgehead on the right bank near Daugavpils (Dvinsk).

On 29 June Timoshenko ordered Kuznetsov to maintain the pressure on the German bridgehead and extra troops were made available. But at the same time Timoshenko insisted that a powerful force be assembled on the old Stalin Line. Confused, Kuznetsov initially assembled these extra troops on the Stalin Line, but believing the German bridgehead to be weakly held he ordered a counterattack. This was spirited but disorganized and was repulsed by the Germans.

In the meantime, to the north 41st Panzer Corps had also reached the Dvina, and immediately 6th Panzer Division set about crossing the river and fighting its way through the first outposts of the Stalin Line. With no reserves to counter this new incursion there was little that Kuznetsov could do to stop the advance; 'In four days of heavy combat, the 6th Panzer Division was the first German unit to fight through the Soviet defences' (Raus, 2002, p.224.)

Worse was to follow for Kuznetsov. By committing his reserve to the defence of the Western Dvina, there was nothing left to hold the Stalin Line. So when the counterattack failed, the old border defences, which had already been stripped of their weapons, were emasculated, and as Machiavelli concluded, 'fortifications without good armies are incompetent for defence'. The Ostrov fortified district fell, and the Pskov and Sebezh fortified regions were also quickly breached but not without a fight. The men of 12th Infantry Division were involved in bitter fighting to capture Point 166 where the defences of the Sebezh Fortified Region were built into the hillside and had to be captured one by one. And even the 3rd SS Panzer Division 'Totenkopf' received something of a bloody nose as it fought its way through the Stalin Line where 'their losses and lack of experience led them … to miss favourable opportunities, and this … caused unnecessary actions to be fought' (Clark, 2001, p.75). The disappointing performance of one of Hitler's elite SS divisions saw it returned to the reserve. In spite of this minor setback the German advance continued apace, and the Soviets were forced to pull back to a new line of defences – the so-called Luga Line.

Army Group Centre

Having smashed through the western border defences, the 2nd and 3rd Panzer armies now advanced on Minsk. The city was protected by two fortified regions that formed a crescent on its western fringe: to the north was the Minsk UR and to the south the Slutsk UR. If Pavlov's armies could be withdrawn in good order and reinforced with reserves now being moved to the front, it should be possible to man these defences and hold the Stalin Line.

Already on 25 June Timoshenko had ordered Pavlov to withdraw his armies from the Bialystok salient, but the order came too late: six divisions had been trapped and the lightning advance of 2nd and 3rd Panzer armies now threatened another even larger encirclement with the jaws snapping shut around Minsk. It was now even more urgent that Pavlov extricate these troops, but the situation was already looking grim.

In spite of the reverses that had befallen the Soviet 4th Army since the first day of the invasion, Major-General A.A. Korobkov was optimistic, not least because his units were almost back at the old Soviet–Polish border and the defences of the Stalin Line. Korobkov had been ordered to man the Slutsk UR and was hopeful that the strong fortifications would provide valuable protection for his battle-weary troops. He sent for the commander of the Slutsk UR to discuss the state of the defences. The report he received was a devastating blow. 'Please keep it in mind,' the man said calmly, 'that all fortifications were abandoned in the beginning of the spring and none has guns now. All our guns were shipped to you at Brest. Now all I have is just one battalion guarding the forts … "And we thought Slutsk would be a good armoured shield," he muttered bitterly' (Pleshakov, 2005, p.138).

The fate of the Soviet 3rd Army to the north of Pavlov's front was equally desperate. Lieutenant-General V.I. Kuznetsov had been pushed back south-eastwards, which opened up a yawning gap with 11th Army (and thus with the North-Western Front). The collapse of the 3rd and 4th armies on either flank of 10th Army left Major-General K.D. Golubev in a precarious situation, and with his units all but out of ammunition 10th Army ceased to be a fighting force. The collapse of the front now exposed Pavlov's second echelon troops. Major-General P.M. Filatov's 13th Army, which had only been formed in May, was responsible for manning the Minsk UR, but with the front disintegrating it was a hopeless task.

With Hoth's 3rd Panzer Army advancing from the north and Guderian's 2nd Panzer Army from the south, the pocket was closed by the end of June with elements of four armies sealed inside (3rd, 4th, 10th and 13th armies). Although Pavlov had left the city, Minsk was still in Soviet hands, and the soon to be replaced commander of the Western Front ordered Filatov to continue holding the Minsk UR, even if encircled. Pavlov confidently predicted that this would not happen, but already German spearheads were racing for the Berezina and any defence of the Minsk UR would be brave but to no avail.

Timoshenko was now aware of the full enormity of the situation and looked to restore a stable line of defence from the River Dvina south to the River Dnieper. In the north the anchor on the Dvina was the Polotsk UR. Timoshenko ordered a 'durable' defence of the Polotsk UR so as to prevent an enemy breakthrough on the right flank of the Western Front. But by early July 20th Panzer Division had already reached the outposts of the Polotsk Fortified Region and was in a position to cross the Western Dvina River and outflank the defences from the south, which it did on 7 July. Meantime 19th Panzer Division and part of the 14th Motorized Division attacked to the north and with this pincer movement effectively bypassed the Polotsk Fortified Region. However, fighting to dislodge the defenders from the fortifications continued. 'Until 16 July units of 174th Rifle Division under Col. Andrei Zygin defended the Polotsk Fortified Region, hampering the progress of ... 18th Motorised Division' (Fugate and Dvoretsky, 1997, p.193). But the resistance was futile.

In spite of the valiant defence of the Polotsk UR, elements of 3rd Panzer Army crossed the River Dvina, and 22nd Army was forced to retreat. This coincided with the capture of the Sebezh Fortified Region to the north, which now meant that a wedge had been driven between the 22nd and 27th armies, but also more significantly between the Western and North-Western fronts. With German bridgeheads on both the Dvina and the Dnieper, Stalin now began to give serious thought to the creation of further defensive lines to protect Moscow (the Vyazma and Mozhaisk lines were constructed, but consisted mainly of field works).

Army Group South

Colonel-General Kirponos continued to defy the Germans. With the defence of the Molotov Line no

This position was built into the arch of a bridge in the Novograd-Volynski Fortified Region. The two loopholes, one on either side, covered the banks of the River Slucz.
(A. Kainaryan)

longer tenable, he oversaw an organized retreat to a line broadly along the old Polish–Soviet border. He now ordered his units to take up positions in the Stalin Line by 9 July. Four of the seven fortified regions in the Kiev Special MD were brought up to nearly full strength. But the reservists who had been rushed forward to man the positions had not had time to familiarize themselves with their positions, or their weapons where they existed. In the other three fortified regions no reserves were forthcoming. In the Korosten Fortified Region, for example, the commandant had only two battalions to hold a front 185km long. This was patently insufficient and he urged the district commanders to send him reinforcements. Some were deployed, but not until the situation just to the south had become critical.

A machine-gun pillbox near the village of Mrygi in the Kiev Fortified Region. In August 1941 the crew of the position was involved in heavy fighting with German units, evidence of which can still be seen. The pillbox was captured after four hours of fighting in which all those inside perished. (A. Kainaryan)

By the beginning of July 13th Panzer Division had reached Slucz, and despite being slowed by the difficult terrain it smashed through the Novograd-Volynski UR and advanced towards Zhitomir, which it captured on 10 July. In its wake tanks of the 14th and 25th Panzer divisions followed to expand the irruption. The armour of 14th Panzer Division found the defences to be more of an obstacle. Forced to remain on the only good road because of torrential rain, which turned the ground into a quagmire, the division advanced towards Zwiahel (Novograd-Volynski). The defences here were constructed in depth and included two *mina* defensive groups. Unable to by pass the defences, the division was 'forced to take the bull by the horns … [It took] the Division five days of heavy fighting to breach the fortifications, seize the town and cross the river' (Glantz, 2004, p.312 – from a report by General der Kavallerie von Mackensen, Commander 3rd Panzer Corps).

This position near Tarasovka in the Kiev Fortified Region originally mounted a 76.2mm M1900 gun (now removed) on a Durliacher caponier mount. This was an open position also known as a TAUT position. (A. Kainaryan)

But the defences were not uniformly strong, as elements of 11th Panzer Division attested. Lieutenant-General H.J. von Hoffgarten, the commander of a motorcycle company and a veteran of the campaign in the west, noted that, 'Contrary to the expectations of our units, the Stalin Line did not prove to be the strongest obstacle against our advance. Certainly there were some bunkers and wire obstacles, but they were far less effective than those which I experienced during the breakthrough of the Maginot Line at Sedan on 13 May 1940' (Glantz, 2004, p. 327).

With the outer ring of defences around Kiev pierced, a series of counterattacks were launched by 5th and 6th armies to close the 'Zhitomir Corridor'. Major-General M.I. Potapov, commander of 5th Army, was responsible for the Korosten Fortified Region and he used it as a springboard for the counterattacks. But neither Potapov nor Lieutenant-General Muzychenko, commander of 6th Army, had sufficient reserves to stem the advance of Kleist's 1st Panzer Army, and it soon became clear that the corridor could not be closed.

The Soviet defenders now fell back in some disarray to the Kiev Fortified Region in an effort to protect the city and prevent the Germans crossing the River Dnieper. The fortified region was reactivated, but there were few mines and little barbed wire to bolster the defences and the troops had insufficient weapons and little ammunition. In spite of this, the line held and for the moment the immediate threat to the Ukrainian capital passed.

Elsewhere the Stalin Line proved more of an obstacle, especially for the infantry. On the left of 1st Panzer Army, Reichenau's 6th Army continued its advance on the River Dnieper. General Maximilian Fretter-Pico's 44th Corps was tasked with breaking through the Stalin Line. The attack was planned for 15 July, but Fretter-Pico was keen to avoid a set-piece attack fearing heavy casualties; so, having identified a weak point in the line, he decided to attack this spot without a preliminary bombardment on 14 July.

The attack was launched by 204th Regiment and, helped by early morning fog and inaccurate enemy fire, the stormtroops managed to secure a foothold in the defences. However, in spite of a feint further north and the surprise nature of the attack, the defenders fought tenaciously to defend their bunkers and each one – 36 in total – had to be destroyed in turn.

To the south of 1st Panzer Army, Stülpnagel's 17th Army continued its drive south-east. By the middle of July 1941, one of its units, 101st Jäger Division, had reached the Stalin Line, and on 15 July 228th Regiment attacked and captured four bunkers. With the bunkers cleared the regiment crossed the River Ljadowa to secure a bridgehead.

The same bunker in the Przemysl Fortified Region as depicted on page 44. This demonstrates that, although the defences did little to slow the German advance, the engagements were often fierce and not without cost in lives lost. (T. Idzikowski)

During 16 July 101st Jäger Division continued to fight its way through the defences, but it was a slow and dangerous job. Often the defenders would vacate their bunkers and take up perfectly camouflaged field positions to assail the enemy attackers. On other occasions they remained in their bunkers and would fight stubbornly to the last man. In one instance German pioneers tried to capture and destroy a bunker, but in spite of numerous attempts the soldiers occupying the position were determined to fight on. Only after six hours of fighting was the bunker eventually captured.

Meantime the troops of 37th Army manning the defences of the Kiev UR continued to resist the German assault. Rather than seize Kiev by frontal assault,

1st Panzer Army swung south-east and along with 17th Army encircled the Soviet 6th and 12th armies at Uman. Kleist's 1st Panzer Army now crossed the River Dnieper near Kremenchug and drove north towards 2nd Panzer Army, which was advancing south. The two met up in the middle of September, trapping 5th and 26th armies and 37th Army protecting Kiev. The city fell soon after, but the troops of 37th Army manning the defences of the Kiev UR had protected the city for over 70 days.

Further south where the Soviet Union shared a border with Romania, the attack did not begin until a week after Operation *Barbarossa*. On 1 July the German 11th Army under Schobert and the Romanian 3rd and 4th armies crossed the River Prut into Soviet-occupied Bessarabia and Bukovina. New defences were planned for this region, but they had not been completed and the composite force soon reached the River Dniester and the old defences of the Stalin Line. On the eastern bank were more than 150 bunkers constructed in three lines, which were manned by troops of Lieutenant-General Smirnov's 18th Army, including 130th and 164th rifle divisions and machine-gun battalions of the 12th Fortified Region.

Early on 17 July lead elements of the Romanian Third Army began to cross the Dniester. Once across, the assault units collected themselves and then attacked the bunkers with a mixture of direct fire from machine guns, anti-tank guns and light artillery and direct assault with explosive charges. By the afternoon the Romanians had captured the first row of bunkers. But now the Soviets put in a series of counterattacks to destroy the bridgehead. These were unsuccessful, as was an attack the following morning, albeit that the bridgehead was reduced in size. From this foothold the Romanians now launched a further attack against the Stalin Line defences and were successful in capturing or destroying 182 pillboxes. But the success of piercing the line had come at a cost, with almost 2,000 men killed or wounded.

All along the front, the border defences had been broken and the Axis forces advanced east. 'In the opinion of Soviet experts, the defensive lines and permanent fortifications established since 1929 at great expense … could have been of great importance and could have represented a serious obstacle to the advancing enemy armies' (Boog, 1998, p.86). However, a series of mistakes and miscalculations meant that the defences were not complete or fully manned, and in spite of a valiant rearguard action they were quickly swept aside by the experienced, well-trained and well-equipped German forces.

AFTERMATH

By the end of 1941 the Axis forces had reached Moscow and all but encircled Leningrad. To the south they were heading towards the River Volga and the city of Stalingrad, which was to be the scene of a momentous struggle and was a turning point in the war. Far to the rear German engineers, as they had done in Belgium and France, made a detailed study of the Soviet border defences. The resulting document, *Denkschrift: uber die russische: Landesbefestigung*, which ran to almost 500 pages, was published in 1942 and provided a snapshot of the fortifications immediately after the line had been captured. It included detailed descriptions of the different bunkers and the weapons and equipment installed, how they were camouflaged and how the bunkers stood up to German fire. It also described the layout of the fortifications and the use of passive defences like obstacles, tank traps and mines.

Soon after the *Denkschrift* had been published, the tide of the war on the Eastern Front turned and the all-conquering Axis forces were forced to retreat. In an effort to stem or at least slow the advance of the Red Army, the Germans, as they did elsewhere, established a series of defensive lines. One of the most significant was the 'Panther Line'. This broadly followed the northern portion of the Stalin Line running along the River Narva, through lakes Peipus and Pskov to Nevel. But the defences of Kingisepp, Pskov and Ostrov had been built to counter an enemy advancing from the west and could not easily be altered to meet the new threat. With few resources and little time to prepare the defences, the Panther Line proved no match for the Soviet forces and was quickly broken. A similar fate befell the German defences constructed in Poland and the renovated 'East Wall' and less than four years after the launch of Operation *Barbarossa* the hammer and sickle flag was flying over the Reichstag in Berlin.

With the war over, the borders in Eastern Europe broadly returned to what they had been before the conflict. Poland and the Baltic States were re-established, albeit that they, and the other satellite states, around the Soviet Union now found themselves under the yoke of communism and effectively governed from Moscow. This buffer zone meant that the Soviet Union no longer needed defences along its western border, but the value of fortifications was still recognized, especially to protect key strategic interests along the borders with China and Finland.

This faith in the value of fortifications seemed to run counter to the experience of Soviet forces in the early part of the war when the Molotov and Stalin Lines did little to slow the Axis attacks. Debate about responsibility for the debacle in 1941, including the critical decision to mothball the defences, were heavily censured after the war. However, in the political manoeuvrings that followed Stalin's death in 1953 some of his potential successors sought to associate their enemies with the crimes and military blunders of the former leader. One example of this was the campaign to tarnish the name of Marshal Georgii Zhukov. After his exploits in delivering victory in the war, the former military commander was extremely popular and had been made defence minister. However, his relationship with Nikita Khrushchev deteriorated and the new leader of the Soviet Union sought to undermine Zhukov's position by linking him with the flawed decision to fortify the new border, even though Zhukov had taken up the post of Chief of the General Staff less than five months before the German invasion. Nevertheless, he was removed from office and sent into exile.

Zhukov was also criticized by Marshal S. Biriuzov, who became Chief of the General Staff in 1963, and by Marshal K. Rokossovskii, a wartime front commander. He believed that the fortifications on the old border should have been maintained and that it was foolish to build a new line under the noses of the Germans and that such an extensive construction could not be completed in time in light of the perilous political situation. Indeed, Rokossovskii's original text was considered too inflammatory for the hyper orthodox Brezhnev regime and it was not until 1989 that the unexpurgated version was published. For his part Zhukov later admitted that he was not happy with the new strategic plan, but he had faith in Stalin's political acumen and to question his judgement too explicitly might have led to his being relieved of his position, or worse.

The period after the war was also characterized by a culture of secrecy. Access to the State Archives was very limited, which meant that until relatively recently *Denkschrift: uber die russische: Landesbefestigung* was the most comprehensive study of the western border defences. However, with the reforms instituted by President Gorbachev, especially the new openness, or *Glasnost*, access to the Russian archives has eased and this has led to a steady stream of articles and books being produced on the subject. Moreover, with the break up of the Soviet Union many of the old defences can now be found in newly independent states like Belarus, Lithuania and Ukraine, where access to them is far less restricted. This has resulted in a further burgeoning of research as historians study the fortifications in their own country.

More recently debate has raged about the fate of the Stalin Line defences after the annexation of Poland in 1939. The question was first raised by the Soviet dissident Petro Grigorenko, a former major-general in the Red Army. He argued that in the period immediately before the German invasion of the Soviet Union, Stalin was massing his forces in the west to attack Germany, and with no further use for the Stalin Line it had been destroyed. His hypothesis was evolved and developed by Viktor Suvorov, a former officer in the Soviet Army, who defected to the United Kingdom where he became a successful writer and historian. He outlined his thoughts on this period in his book *Icebreaker*, which included a section on the destruction of the Stalin Line.

However, while it is true that many of the defences were abandoned and often stripped of their equipment and weapons, there is no evidence to suggest that the defences were systematically destroyed. The Germans found in excess of 3,000 emplacements, which if not fully operational were considered 'combat capable'. An appreciation by German Army intelligence staff after the fighting described the Stalin Line as a 'dangerous combination of concrete, field works and natural obstacles, tank traps, mines, marshy belts around forts, artificial lakes enclosing defences, cornfields cut according to the trajectory of machine gun fire. Its whole extent right up to the positions of the defenders was camouflaged with a consummate art' (Clark, 2001, p.31).

The German appreciation is reinforced by Soviet evidence from the time. In June 1941 the chief engineer in the Baltic MD noted that almost 200 emplacements were capable of being manned in the Pskov, Ostrov and Sebezh fortified regions. In the Western MD, a study the previous September found the defences of the Minsk Fortified Region were still in situ, albeit that 'the

Soldiers help to clear artillery bunker No. 134. This was later fully restored and now forms part of the Stalin Line Museum at Zaslavl near Minsk. Even at this early stage of restoration it is possible to see the armoured shield and opening for the winch cable. (E. Hitriak and I. Volkov)

emplacements and the equipment removed from them were in deplorable condition' (Tarleton, 1993, p.44). In the Kiev fortified area the defences were without weapons and overgrown, but they were still there and a significant number of emplacements also survived in the Korosten and Novograd-Volynski fortified areas (c. 650), albeit that they too were undoubtedly in a poor state. And if further evidence were needed it is still possible to see many of the defences today.

THE SITES TODAY

In the post-war years the defences of the Stalin and Molotov lines were ignored, scattered as they were in the vast spaces of the former Soviet Union. Ironically this neglect ensured that many of the fortifications survived, whereas in Western Europe post-war development and safety concerns saw many destroyed or buried.

Following the break up of the Soviet Union there were major changes to the western border region, which saw the restoration of states that had not enjoyed independence since well before the war. This momentous change means that today the remains of the Stalin and Molotov lines can be found in at least eight different countries: Belarus, Finland, Lithuania, Moldova, Poland, Romania, Russia and Ukraine. These countries are not perhaps in most people's top ten holiday destinations, but the fact that they are less familiar in many ways makes a visit more attractive, and also something of a challenge. The majority of the fortifications are located in four countries.

Belarus

Belarus has examples of defences of both the Molotov and Stalin lines within its borders. The defences of the former can be found along the frontier with Poland while those of the latter are located to the west of Minsk. Some of the defences were destroyed in the war, but many are still intact and a unique group have been restored and form the basis of the Stalin Line Museum just outside Minsk.

The museum was opened in June 2005 to mark the 60th anniversary of the victory of the Soviet people in the Great Patriotic War. It is based around a company command sector of the Minsk Fortified Region and includes four bunkers: two machine-gun bunkers – Nos. 132 and 292, a half-caponier with 76.2mm guns – No. 134 and a command bunker, No. 135. The bunkers have been restored to their original state with original weapons, ventilation and cooling systems and communication equipment. The damage to the shelters suffered in the fighting of 1941 has been left.

As well as the original fortifications, there is a small collection of Russian, Polish and German armoured turrets – including an emplaced T26 tank turret and an MG Panzernest – taken from various locations in Belarus to save them from scrap metal merchants.

Each of the 76.2mm M1902 guns in the half-caponier bunkers of the Stalin Line were protected by large armoured plates that could be raised and lowered on steel cables. Here the armoured flap has been lowered enabling the weapon to fire. This bunker formed part of the Minsk Fortified Region and now has been fully restored and is open to the public as part of the Stalin Line Museum. (Author's photograph)

A series of field works and communication trenches have also been constructed to original wartime designs, as have passive anti-tank and anti-infantry defences including steel hedgehogs and wire entanglements.

In spite of its name the Stalin Line Museum does not simply concentrate on defences of the war. In addition it houses a large collection of tanks, military vehicles, artillery, engineer equipment, aircraft and helicopters from various periods. The museum also plays host to a series of battle recreations at different times of the year.

The museum is 26km from Minsk and 6km from Zaslavl and can be found on the Minsk–Molodechno road. It is open every day (except Monday) from 10am until 6pm and there is plenty of parking. A small café serves food and drinks. (Contact details: e-mail:info@stalin-line.by, web: www.stalin-line.by)

In addition to the Stalin Line Museum there is a pillbox museum in Borisov as well as numerous other positions that can be visited. Belarus also has a number of other sites of interest. One worthy of mention is the fortress at Brest, which can be combined with a visit to the Brest Fortified Region. The fortress was the scene of fierce fighting during the German invasion of Poland in September 1939 and during Operation *Barbarossa* when the garrison held out against overwhelming odds for more than two weeks. Although badly damaged in the fighting, significant portions remain and a museum has been created for visitors while in the centre there is an impressive memorial to the fallen heroes.

Poland

Following the invasion of Poland in September 1939, and in accordance with the Nazi–Soviet Non Aggression Pact, Poland was partitioned. The Soviets decided to fortify the new border. Today many of these defences are still located in modern-day Poland and it is possible to visit fortifications in the Brest, Przemysl, Rava-Russkaia and Zambruv fortified regions, but there are no museums dedicated to the subject.

The defences of the Przemysl Fortified Region are interspersed with the 19th-century fortifications that were constructed in two rings around the city.

The restored bridge leading across the River Mukhavets to the Kholmskie Gate of the Brest Fortress. This was the scene of heavy fighting in June 1941, as demonstrated by the damage to the buildings. Unlike the more modern fortifications the garrison of the 19th-century fortress held out for some weeks before being captured by the Germans. (Author's photograph)

In World War I Russian forces encircled them and many were later destroyed. However, many can still be visited and there is a small museum – Museum Twierdzy Przemysl at ul. Grodzka 8.

Russia

Russia is still home to many of the defences of the Stalin Line, especially those built in the Leningrad MD. Again there are no museums specifically dedicated to the defences of the Stalin and Molotov lines, but it is possible to visit the Central Museum of the Great Patriotic War, located in Victory Square in Moscow and the Artillery, Sappers and Signals Museum in St Petersburg, both of which include some fortifications. A number of bunkers in the Stalin Line have also been transformed into memorials and can be visited, but they are not always easy to find.

While visiting Moscow and St Petersburg it is also possible to visit the defences of the Luga and Leningrad lines around St Petersburg and the Mozhaisk Line around Moscow. The latter protected the capital, and one bunker at Ilinskoye has been transformed into a memorial to the students of the Podolsk Military College who perished there.

Of course the two great cities of Russia also have many other attractions including Red Square and the Hermitage as well as lesser-known attractions to those interested in fortifications, like the fortresses at Kronstadt and Oreshek.

ABOVE A half-caponier mounting two 76.2mm guns on L17 mount and a Maxim machine gun which formed part of the Stare Brusno Position in the Rava-Russkaia Fortified Region. Below each of the embrasures it is possible to see the opening for the spent shell cases. The middle 76.2mm gun was removed using explosives after the war and is now on display at the Polish Army Museum, Warsaw. (Author's photograph)

A bunker in the city of Przemysl that covered the River San. Both loopholes were badly damaged in the fighting of June 1941 – see photo on page 60 – but this was repaired after the war and at one point the roof of the bunker was used as a terrace for drinkers. (Author's photograph)

Ukraine

Like Belarus, the Ukraine is blessed with a number of fortified regions from both the Molotov and Stalin lines, but unlike Belarus there is no large museum devoted to the subject. There is a small museum in the 'Skelya' command bunker, and visitors can also visit the many bunkers in the various fortified regions.

The Ukraine is also home to many other castles and fortresses like Khotin, Kamenets Podolski and Palanok or Mukachevo Castle. The capital, Kiev, is also beautiful and has many other places of interest.

General information

When considering visiting the defences of the Stalin and Molotov lines it is important to take certain precautions. Access to the bunkers is generally straightforward because there is easy public access. However, they are often located in dense forest and it is therefore better to visit the sites in the spring or autumn when the undergrowth is less of a problem, and whenever possible take a local guide.

Inside the structures there are many dangers including holes in the floor where trap doors have been removed. There are also trip hazards and low doorways and other obstructions that can lead to serious injuries. There is also sadly the modern menace of rubbish that is not only unpleasant but also brings with it other health hazards. For these reasons it is essential that you take a light with spare batteries and do not travel alone.

Travel

All of the major cities in countries where the main fortifications are located are served by regular flights from the UK and the US and increasingly there are also flights to regional airports that are often located nearer to the defences.

For the slightly more intrepid traveller it is also possible to take the train. Much of Eastern Europe is covered by an extensive rail network, albeit that the gauge in Russia is different to that in the rest of Europe, which involves a change of bogies on the border – an experience in itself.

It is also possible to drive to the defences. However, it is important to remember the great distances between the different fortified regions and that the roads are often not good; as such, great care should be taken driving at night and in bad weather. Motorists should also be aware that there may be long queues at the border, and that customs and immigration can be lengthy and bureaucratic, especially in the former Soviet Union.

OPPOSITE PAGE, BOTTOM
The remains of an M1 pillbox near Mrygi in the Kiev Fortified Region. Originally this would have housed three machine guns. In August 1941 the crew of the bunker blew up the position and it is now a memorial to those who died. (A. Kainaryan)

A Soviet bunker of the Molotov Line that formed part of the Przemysl Fortified Region. The embrasures have received at least one direct hit each from German guns. On top of the bunker German soldiers are constructing simple flak emplacements. (T. Idzikowski)

Driving licences issued by any EU member state are mutually recognized in other EU member states, but you should carry original vehicle registration papers, ownership documents and insurance papers at all times. This is also true for the countries of the former Soviet Union where, as a foreign driver, you may additionally be asked to pay a fee.

Although many of the countries where the fortifications are located are not renowned for tourism, accommodation of all types is generally plentiful, especially in the major cities.

Entry requirements

Visas are required to enter or transit Russia or Belarus and without one you may be fined or refused entry. A migration card must also be completed on entry and additionally visitors staying more than three days must register with the local authorities, although the hotel will normally arrange this.

Visas are not required for the Ukraine or Moldova if you are an EU citizen (provided you are staying less than 90 days), but you may need to register with the local authorities when you arrive at your destination. Those countries that now form part of the wider European Union (Finland, Lithuania, Poland, Romania) generally have few or no entry requirements save for a valid UK or US passport.

Currency

In the former Soviet Union ATMs are available, but are less numerous than in the west. Similarly, credit cards are not widely used, although some large stores and restaurants will take them. Travellers are therefore advised to take sufficient cash to cover living costs for the duration of their stay, but before travelling check exchange control regulations for each country. US dollars and euros can be readily exchanged in major cities (sterling is less widely accepted), but travellers should use only official exchange booths.

Language

Although English is spoken in many of the countries it is not as widely used as in much of Western Europe. It should also be remembered that many of the defences are located in the former Soviet Union and as such Russian is the most widely used language and the Cyrillic alphabet is used.

Photography
In the former Soviet Union as a general rule you should avoid taking photographs of all government buildings, military installations and uniformed officials. As such it is advisable to take extreme care photographing fortifications when they are located in border zones.

BIBLIOGRAPHY

PRIMARY SOURCES

Russian State Military Archive
Rossiyskiy Gosudarstvenniy Voenniy Arkhiv (RGVA),
    Fond 22, Opis 32, Delo 2595
RGVA, Fond 36967, Opis 1, Delo 54, pages 26–34
RGVA, Fond 36967, Opis 1, Delo 80
RGVA, Fond 36967, Opis 1, Delo 410

SECONDARY SOURCES

Berchin, M. and Ben Horin, E. *The Red Army*
    (London, 1942).
Boog, H. *Deutsche Reich und der Zweite Weltkrieg*,
    Vol. 4: *Attack on the Soviet Union* (Clarendon,
    Oxford, 1998).
Clark, A. *Barbarossa – The Russian German Conflict
    1941–1945* (Cassell, London, 2001).
Erickson, J. *The Soviet High Command – A Military-
    Political History 1918–1941* (Frank Cass,
    London, 2001).
Erickson, J. *The Road to Stalingrad – Stalin's War with
    Germany*, Vol. 1 (Cassell, London, 2003).
Fugate, B. and Dvoretsky, L. *Thunder on the Dnepr*
    (Presidio, Novato, California, 1997).
Glantz, D.M. *Stumbling Colossus: the Red Army on the
    Eve of World War II* (University Press of Kansas,
    Lawrence, 1998).
Glantz, D.M., *The Battle for Leningrad: 1941–1944*
    (University Press of Kansas, Lawrence, 2002).
Glantz, D.M., *The Initial Period of the War on the
    Eastern Front 22 June – August 1941 – Proceedings
    of the Fourth Art of War Symposium – Garmisch,
    October 1987* (Frank Cass, Abingdon, Oxon, 2004).
Glantz, D.M. *The Military Strategy of the Soviet Union
    – A History* (Frank Cass, Abingdon, Oxon, 2004).
Kaufmann, J.E. and Jurga, R.M. *Fortress Europe –
    European Fortifications in World War II* (Combined
    Publishing, Pennsylvania, 1999).
Pleshakov, K. *Stalin's Folly : the Tragic First Ten Days
    of World War II on the Eastern Front* (Houghton
    Mifflin, Boston, 2005).
Raus, E. *Fighting in Hell : the German Ordeal on the
    Eastern Front* (Greenhill Books, London, 1995).

Raus, E. *Panzers on the Eastern Front: General Erhard
    Raus and his Panzer Divisions in Russia 1941-1945*
    (Greenhill Books, London, 2002).
Ritgen, Oberst a.D.H., *The 6th Panzer Division
    1937–45* (Osprey Publishing, London, 1988).
Seaton, A. *The Russo-German War 1941–45*
    (Presidio, Novato, California, 1990).
Suvorov, V. *Icebreaker: Who Started World War II?*
    (Hamish Hamilton, London, 1990).
Werth, A. *Russia at War 1941–45* (Pan, London, 1965).
Wesolowski, T. *Linia Molotowa, Sowieckie Fortyfikacje
    Graniczne Z Lat 1940-41 Na Przykladzie 62
    Brzeskiego Rejonu Umocnionego* (Instytut Historii
    Uniwersytetu w Bialymstoku, Bialystok, 2001).
Zhukov, G, *Reminiscences and Reflections* (Progress
    Publishers, Moscow, 1985).

ARTICLES

Denkschrift: uber die russische: Landesbefestigung 1942
Department of the Army Pamphlet No. 20-269,
    *Small Unit Actions during the German Campaign
    in Russia.*
Gavrilkin, N.V. '76mm Casemate Artillery Mount
    M.1940 (L-17)', Moscow.
Kaminski, V., 'Permanent Land Front of USSR
    (1927-1939) *Redoubt* No. 1 2006.
Khorkov, A. 'Fortified regions on the USSR western
    borders' *Voenno-istoricheskiy* Journal No.12 1987.
Shmunevsky, P. and Kuziak, A. 'Mina of Gulsk' *Polygon*
    No. 3 (11) 2002.
Sidorov, Col. V., 'Fortified Areas: Lessons and
    Conclusions' *Voyennyy Vestnik* No. 4 April 1991.
Svirin, M. 'Why did Stalin destroy the Stalin Line?'
    Polygon No. 3 (11) 2002.
Tarleton, R. 'What Really Happened to the Stalin Line?'
    Part I *The Journal of Soviet Military Studies*
    (June 1992) Vol. 5 No. 2 p. 187–219.
Tarleton, R. 'What Really Happened to the Stalin Line?'
    Part II *The Journal of Slavic Military Studies*
    (March 1993) Vol. 6 No. 1 p. 21-61.
Various, 'Historical Fortification Collection of Articles'
    Fortress Russia Issue 2, 2005.

GLOSSARY

Batal'onnye raiony oborony	Battalion defence region.
Boyevoe sooruzheniye	Fighting post.
Caponier	A fortification positioned so that fire can be brought to bear on both flanks.
Casemate	Chamber inside a fortification for protecting personnel and weapons.
Centre of resistance	The name for a Battalion defence region after 1938.
Embrasure	Opening for weapon to be fired.
Fortified region	See UR.
Glavnoe Voenno-Inzhenernoe Upravleniia	Defence Commissariat's Main Military Engineering Directorate.
Half-caponier	A fortification where fire can only be brought to bear on one flank.
Komandnyi punkt	Command post.
Komitet Oborony	Defence Committee.
Komitet po injenernoi podgoptovke teatrov voennyh dejstvii	Committee for the Engineering Preparation of the Theatres of Military Action.
Nabludatelnyi punkt	Observation post.
Narkom-voenmor	People's Commissar for Military and Naval Affairs.
NIOP AU US RKKA	Nauchnoispytatelnyi orujeinyi polygon Artilleriiskogo upravleniia: Scientific Proving Ground of the Artillery Directorate.
NKO	People's Commissariat of Defence.
NKVD	Narodny Kommissariat Vnutrennikh Del: People's Commissariat for Internal Affairs.
Ognevaya tochka	Frontal firing.
Opornye punkty	Strongpoints.
Orudiyno-pulemetnyi polukaponir	Artillery and MG half-caponier.
Osobyi	Special.
Otdel stroitelstva kapitalnyh oboronitelnyh soorujenii	Department for the Construction of Permanent Defensive Installations.
Poduchastki	Subsector of a UNR.
Polosa obespecheniia (sometimes termed *Predpol'e*)	Forward defence zone.
Postanovleie	Special decree.
Predpol'e	See *Polosa obespecheniia*.
Protivotankovaya ognevaya tochka	Anti-tank firing post.
RKKA	Robochiy Krestyanskaya Krasnaya Armiya: The Workers and Peasants Red Army, or simply the Red Army.
RRO	Rotnyi rayon oborony: company defence region. A smaller independent version of the battalion defence region.
RUO	Rotnyi uchastok oborony: company defence area. A subdivision of the battalion defence region.
RVS	*Revvoensoviet*:Revolutionary Military Soviet.
Specialnaya Inspekciya Inzhenernykh Voysk	Special Inspectorate of Engineering Troops.

Stavka	*Stavka Glavnogo Komandovaniya*: High Command Headquarters.
Strongpoint	The name for a company defence region after 1938.
TOT	*Tankovaya ognievaya totshka*: Tank turret.
Ubezhische	Shelter.
Uchastki	Sector or site of the UNR.
UNI VSU RKKA	*Upravleniia Nachal'nika Ingenerov Voenno-stroitelnogo upravleniia*: Directorate of Chief Engineers of the Military Construction Directorate.
UNR	*Upravleniia nachal'nika rabot*: Labour directorate.
UNVSR	Upravleniia Nachal'nika Voennostroitel'nyh: Military Labour Directorate.
Upravleniia Oboronitel'nogo Stroitel'stva	Directorate of Defensive Construction.
UP	*Ukreplinnyje polosa*: Fortified zone.
UR	*Ukreplinnyje rajony*: Fortified region. This can signify either the system of fortifications in an area or the specialist unit assigned to man the defences.
VoHimU	Voenno-Himicheskoe Upravleniia: Military Chemical Directorate.
VSU RKKA	Voenno-Stroitelnoe Upravleniia: Military Construction Directorate of the RKKA.
VTU	Voenno-Tehnicheskoe Upravleniia: Military Technical Directorate.

APPENDIX: RED ARMY ORDER OF BATTLE, 22 JUNE 1941

NORTHERN
7th Army
26th Fortified Region (Sortavala)
14th Army
23rd Fortified Region (Murmansk)
23rd Army
27th Fortified Region (Keksholm)
28th Fortified Region (Vyborg)

Front
21st Fortified Region
22nd Fortified Region (Karelia)
25th Fortified Region (Pskov)
29th Fortified Region (Pskov)

NORTH-WESTERN
8th Army
44th Fortified Region (Kaunas)
48th Fortified Region (Alytus)
11th Army
42nd Fortified Region (Shiauliai)
45th Fortified Region (Telshiai)
46th Fortified Region (Telshiai)

Front
41st Fortified Region (Libava) – naval
base in Latvia

WESTERN
3rd Army
68th Fortified Region (Grodno)
4th Army
62nd Fortified region (Brest)
10th Army
66th Fortified Region (Osovets)

Front
58th Fortified Region (Sebezh)
61st Fortified Region (Polotsk)
63rd Fortified Region
  (Minsk – Slutsk)
64th Fortified Region (Zambruv)
65th Fortified Region (Mozyr)

SOUTH-WESTERN
5th Army
2nd Fortified Region (Vladimir-
  Volynski)
6th Army
4th Fortified Region (Strumilov)
6th Fortified Region
  (Rava-Russkaia)
12th Army
10th Fortified Region (Kamenets-
  Podolski)

11th Fortified Region
  (Mogilev-Podolski)
12th Fortified Region
  (Mogilev-Podolski)
26th Army
8th Fortified Region

Front
1st Fortified Region (Kiev)
3rd Fortified Region (Letichev)
5th Fortified Region (Korosten)
7th Fortified Region (Novograd-
  Volynski)
13th Fortified Region (Shepetovka)
15th Fortified Region (Ostropol)
17th Fortified Region (Iziaslavl)

9TH SEPARATE ARMY
80th Fortified Region (Rybnitsa)
81st Fortified Region (Danube)
82nd Fortified Region (Tiraspol)
84th Fortified Region (Verkhne-Prut)
86th Fortified Region (Nizhne-Prut)

ODESSA MD
83rd Fortified Region

INDEX